The U.S. Navy
Pictorial History
of the War of 1812

The U.S. Navy Pictorial History of the War of 1812

Don Philpott

ROWMAN & LITTLEFIELD PUBLISHERS, INC.
Lanham • Boulder • New York • Toronto • Plymouth, UK

Published by Rowman & Littlefield Publishers, Inc.
A wholly owned subsidiary of The Rowman & Littlefield Publishing Group, Inc.
4501 Forbes Boulevard, Suite 200, Lanham, Maryland 20706
www.rowman.com

10 Thornbury Road, Plymouth PL6 7PP, United Kingdom

British Library Cataloguing in Publication Information Available

Library of Congress Cataloging-in-Publication Data
Philpott, Don, 1946–
The U.S. Navy pictorial history of the War of 1812 / Don Philpott.
p. cm.
Includes bibliographical references and index.
ISBN 978-1-4422-1907-6 (cloth : alk. paper) — ISBN 978-1-4422-1908-3 (electronic)
1. United States—History—War of 1812. 2. United States. Navy—History—War of 1812.
3. United States—History—War of 1812—Pictorial works. 4. United States. Navy—
History—War of 1812—Pictorial works. I. Title.
E354.P55 2012
973.5'2—dc23   2012007097

♾™ The paper used in this publication meets the minimum requirements of American
National Standard for Information Sciences—Permanence of Paper for
Printed Library Materials, ANSI/NISO Z39.48-1992.

Printed in the United States of America

CONTENTS

ACKNOWLEDGMENTS

THIS BOOK would not have been possible without the support of the U.S. Naval History and Heritage Command. In particular, the author would like to acknowledge Captain Daniel Dayton and Captain Chris Christopher for their support, knowledge, enthusiasm, and friendship. The author would also like to thank Gale Munro, head curator of the Navy Art Collection, for her assistance with the paintings and prints that have been used.

A great deal of the information for this book has been gathered from public domain sources, in particular the archives of the Navy's History and Heritage Command based at the Washington Navy Yard, which saw action during the War of 1812. Its website commemorating the war can be found at www.history.navy.mil/commemorations/1812/1812-index .htm. The author also relied heavily throughout on the following two works: *The Reestablishment of the Navy,* by Michael Crawford and Christine E. Hughes, Naval History Biographies, No. 4, published by the Naval Historical Center, Department of the Navy; and *The War of 1812,* extracted from American Military History, Army Historical Series, Office of the Chief of Military History, U.S. Army.

Introduction

THE WAR OF 1812 has been called the Second War of American Independence. Fought between the United States and Great Britain (with France acting as a thorn in both their sides), the war lasted for four years and included many major land and sea battles. The British blockaded the U.S. Atlantic coast and launched several major attacks. They captured Washington, D.C., and burned the Capitol and much of the rest of the city. The Americans raided Canada. The heroic defense of Fort McHenry inspired the U.S. national anthem, "The Star-Spangled Banner." However, for much of the war, neither side could claim major victories or retain any land gained.

A peace treaty was signed in Ghent, Belgium, on December 25, 1814, yet because of the time taken to ratify it and get the word back to America, the war continued for another five months. When it ended,

Bombardment of Fort McHenry (engraving by W. M. Kneass)

USS *Constitution* in Action against HMS *Guerriere*
(Thomas Birch, engraving by Cornelius Tiebout)

each participant declared victory. The British claimed the war opened the way to a new era of trade and prosperity with the United States. Canada found a new spirit of nationalism that led to the unification of Lower and Upper Canada. The war firmly established the United States as a new major naval power and a political force, and it shaped the United States into what we know today. Had the British won the Battle of New Orleans, they would have controlled most land west of the Mississippi, thus discouraging westward expansion for the fledgling country. Today's United States would not exist.

The war also spurred the establishment of the U.S. Navy. While this book commemorates the bicentenary of the 1812 war, it also celebrates the emergence and growth of the U.S. Navy. "Without a Respectable Navy," wrote Captain John Paul Jones of the Continental Navy early in the American Revolutionary War, "Alas America!"

ONE

STORM CLOUDS BUILDING: 1803–1812

TENSIONS MOUNTED between the United States, Great Britain, and France in the decade prior to the War of 1812. Britain's war with Napoleon led to trade restrictions on the United States, as the British tried to keep the Americans from trading with France. These restrictions were motivated not only by the war with France but also by growing concern in Great Britain over the expansion of the U.S. Navy. To be sure, the British did not want American ships supplying goods to France and hindering the war effort. But the growth of the U.S. Navy posed a threat to Britain's maritime dominance and its position as the world's trading superpower.

The prewar trade restrictions—which the United States contested as illegal under international law—accompanied aggressive British battleship patrols off the U.S. Atlantic coast. Harsh conditions aboard ships caused many sailors to desert when they went ashore, leaving most vessels undermanned. The Royal Navy overcame its labor shortage by impressment: Upon boarding a vessel, they would appropriate what men they needed and "recruit" them into the Royal Navy. Press gangs of naval officers and Royal Marines would scour ports looking for men to take aboard—whether they had seagoing experience or not. They plied men with alcohol until the men passed out, or simply knocked them unconscious, and carried them aboard ship. By the time the new recruits woke up, the ship had sailed. Thus they found themselves unwilling sailors in the Royal Navy.

The Battle of Trafalgar (J. M. W. Turner)

At the beginning of the nineteenth century, about half the crew members on Royal Navy ships had been impressed. The Royal Navy paid these involuntary recruits less than regular sailors and kept them in chains when the ship was in port. Because of the war with France, Britain needed to staff as many ships as possible—so impressment increased. An estimated six thousand American seamen were impressed into British service.

In 1805, on the excuse of searching for deserters, the Royal Navy started to board American merchant ships. Whether they found deserters or not, the British impressed the crew and took possession of both the ship and its cargo. Scores of U.S. ships and their crews were absorbed into the Royal Navy this way.

On June 22, 1807, the British warship HMS *Leopard* attacked and boarded the American frigate *Chesapeake* off the coast of Norfolk, Virginia. The *Leopard* had blockaded the mouth of Chesapeake Bay to prevent two French warships from leaving when it learned that several

Caricature of a Press Gang

Royal Navy deserters had joined the crew of the *Chesapeake*. The captain of the *Leopard* hailed the *Chesapeake* and asked to send over a search party to look for deserters. When the *Chesapeake's* captain, Commodore James Barron, refused, the *Leopard* opened fire with all guns, crippling the *Chesapeake*, killing three American sailors, and injuring eighteen, including the captain. The *Leopard's* boarding party found four Royal Navy deserters, one British born, the other three U.S. citizens. "The British deserter was hanged from the yardarm of his ship, and the Americans were each sentenced to 500 lashes."[1] However, the incident caused such an outcry that the British government released the men and agreed to pay reparations for the damage to the *Chesapeake*.[2]

But the American people clamored for war. The U.S. government demanded that the British withdraw from U.S. territorial waters and end impressment of sailors aboard U.S. vessels. The British declined (although they did eventually end impressment in 1814).

---

1. Nathan Miller, *The U.S. Navy: A History* (Annapolis, MD: Naval Institute Press, 1997), 57.

2. Commodore Barron was relieved of his command and suspended from the navy for five years by a committee of inquiry. In 1813, the British frigate HMS *Shannon* captured the *Chesapeake* off Boston. For the next seven years, the *Chesapeake* flew under the flag of the Royal Navy. In 1820, Barron killed Commodore Stephen Decatur in a duel over comments he had made about the 1807 incident. Barron was not charged, and he continued to serve in the navy, becoming its most senior officer in 1839.

Commodore Stephen Decatur
(oil on canvas by V. Zveg)

USS *Chesapeake* and HMS *Shannon*
(print by M. Corne, engraving by Wightman)

Thomas Jefferson (portrait by Rembrandt Peale)

War was also fueled by British support for Native Americans. British traders armed tribes in Canada and encouraged them to fight the Americans along the northwest frontier to discourage U.S. expansion into tribal lands. The British wanted to create a vast neutral Indian buffer state that would have covered Ohio, Indiana, and Michigan and prevented further U.S. expansion. They continued to press their demand even at the peace talks in 1814. By then, however, they had few bargaining chips, and the proposal was rejected.

The Canadians entered the war reluctantly. Many living in Upper Canada (now Ontario) were recent emigrants from America—exiled for maintaining allegiance to the British crown after the Revolutionary War. To avoid being annexed by the United States, they took up arms to protect themselves. Yet the majority of Americans thought Canada would be an easy conquest. Thomas Jefferson wrote in 1812, "The acquisition

Benjamin Stoddert
(portrait by E. F. Andrews)

of Canada this year, as far as the neighborhood of Quebec, will be a mere matter of marching, and will give us the experience for the attack on Halifax, the next and final expulsion of England from the American continent."

France was embroiled with Britain in the Napoleonic Wars, which started in 1793 and would end in 1815. The United States, a neutral nation, could freely do business with any country, but both Britain and France interfered with this free trade. The French were anxious to receive goods from America, but their navy nevertheless boarded many American ships and confiscated vessel, crew, and cargo.

Secretary of the Navy Benjamin Stoddert

realized that the infant Navy possessed too few warships to protect a far-flung merchant marine by using convoys or by patrolling the North

American coast. Rather, he concluded that the best way to defeat the French campaign against American shipping was by offensive operations in the Caribbean, where most of the French cruisers were based.[3]

When Stoddert became secretary of the navy in 1798, only one American naval vessel was deployed in what became known as the Quasi-War. By the end of the year, a force of twenty ships was planned for the Caribbean. Before the hostilities ended, the force available to the U.S. Navy approached thirty vessels, with some seven hundred officers and five thousand seamen. The British assisted by selling stores and munitions to the American navy.

The brief Quasi-War ended in 1800 with a peace treaty. But it had

highlighted several weaknesses in the fledgling navy, both in the shore establishment and in the operational forces. Problems arose in procurement, provisioning, manning of ships, delegation of authority, and planning for an extensive campaign. Squadron commanders learned that they required smaller ships to pursue enemy privateers in shallow waters. Many of the merchantmen converted into men-of-war proved to be poor sailers.[4]

In 1806, the French, still at war with Britain, enacted the Continental Blockade, which banned all France's allies and all those countries under the rule of France from doing business with the British. The plan was to isolate Britain, prevent trade in or out, and cause the country to collapse—at which point Napoleon would send over his invasion army. But Napoleon's navy was not large or powerful enough to enforce the blockade: English traders continued to receive imports by sea and to trade with the Continent.

Britain retaliated in 1807 with its Orders in Council, prohibiting any of its trading partners from doing business with France or any of its allies. The United States responded by passing the Embargo Act of 1807, banning most overseas trade. President Jefferson thought that this would

3. U.S. Naval History and Heritage Command, Benjamin Stoddert (1751-1813), First Secretary of the Navy, *Biographies in Naval History*, http://www.history.navy.mil/bios/stoddert.htm.

4. Michael J. Crawford and Christine E. Hughes, *The Reestablishment of the Navy, 1787–1801: Historical Overview and Select Bibliography*, Naval History Biographies, No. 4 (Washington, DC: Naval Historical Center, Department of the Navy, 1995), 10.

Action between U.S. Frigate *Constellation* and French Frigate *Insurgente*,
February 9, 1799 (painting by Rear Admiral John W. Schmidt)

protect America's interests and not draw the country into a war. However, its primary effect was to hurt U.S. merchants who lost their trade because overseas merchants, including the British, continued to ship their goods to America and elsewhere. Eventually U.S. traders simply ignored the embargo and took to smuggling.

In 1809, the Embargo Act was repealed. But the following year, France agreed to stop attacking American ships. As part of that accord, America reinstated its trading embargo with Britain. Now war was inevitable.

TIME LINE OF MAJOR EVENTS LEADING TO THE WAR OF 1812

1803

May 18. War resumes between Great Britain and the First French Empire. The British warn the Americans not to trade with France or its colonies.

1804

November 3. Quashquame, a Sauk chief, leads a delegation to St. Louis to hand over lands in western Illinois and northeast Missouri to the U.S. government. It is later argued that the Sauk and Meskwaki delegation had no authority to sign treaties, having been sent to hand over a murder suspect and make amends for the killing. This dispute will cause many Sauk, including Black Hawk, to side with the British during the War of 1812.

1805

May 22. The British Admiralty issues the *Essex* **Decision**, ruling that American merchant ships cannot avoid British trade restrictions by calling into a U.S. port. This decision follows the capture of the *Essex*, an American merchant ship, which claimed that it did not directly trade with the French because it interrupted its voyage by visiting a U.S. port. The British ruling gives the Royal Navy increased power to seize neutral ships.

October 21. Admiral Lord Nelson defeats the French and Spanish fleets at the **Battle of Trafalgar**, off the southwest coast of Spain. Although the victory establishes the Royal Navy's dominance of the seas, it has little impact on the land war between Britain and France, which rages for another ten years. However, it does cause problems for the neutral Americans, whose merchant ships are now more vulnerable.

1806

April 18. In retaliation against the British, who continue to impress neutral American merchant seamen, the U.S. Congress passes the **Nonimportation Act,** banning the import of a number of British goods. It has little impact.

November 21. The **Berlin Decree** is issued by Napoleon, banning the import of all British goods into Europe.

December 31. The United States and Britain sign the **Monroe-Pinkney Treaty** in an effort to end the impressment of American merchant ships and their crews and to have America's neutrality recognized. President Jefferson does not receive the treaty until March 1807 and refuses to submit it to Congress for ratification. (Britain likely would not have honored the treaty in any case, as they were desperate for sailors in their war with France.)

1807

June 22. The *Chesapeake-Leopard* **Affair** results in the crippling of the USS *Chesapeake.*

November 11. The British government issues the **Orders in Council,** a series of decrees aimed at hindering the French war effort by banning all trade with France and implementing a naval blockade to enforce it. This further strains the U.S. relationship with Britain.

December 17. Napoleon retaliates with the **Milan Decree,** prohibiting any European country from trading with Britain. The decree also authorizes French warships to seize any ships sailing to or from British ports.

December 22. The United States responds with the **Embargo Act.** As part of President Jefferson's efforts to avoid war at all costs, the Embargo Act prohibits American ships from sailing to foreign ports. Jefferson argues that neither Britain nor France would have an excuse for attacking the United States or its vessels if they were not trading overseas. Despite congressional attempts to close loopholes, many American merchant ships ignore the act and resort to smuggling. Its main effect, rather, is near disaster for the United States financially as crops and goods cannot be sold abroad.

James Madison
(portrait by J. Vanderlyn)

1808

April 17. Napoleon issues the **Bayonne Decree**, arguing that because American ships have been ordered not to trade overseas, any vessels flying the U.S. flag must be British ships under false colors and should therefore be seized. As a result, more than three hundred American vessels are captured.

1809

March 1. The **Non-Intercourse Act**, signed by Jefferson in the last days of his presidency, replaces the Embargo Act. This act allows American ships to sail anywhere other than British or French ports. However, it is no more effective than the Embargo Act and further damages the U.S. economy.

March 4. **James Madison**, who was Jefferson's secretary of state from 1801 to 1809, is inaugurated as the nation's fourth president. Under his presidency, the people become increasingly angry with the British and hungry for war, and they elect the "War Hawks" leadership to Congress in 1811. Madison has two choices: make a deal with Britain or declare war. He chooses the former.

April 19. The **Erskine Agreement**, an attempt to normalize trade between the United States and Britain, is signed. Under the terms of the agreement, negotiated between David Erskine, the British minister to the United States, and President Madison, America agrees to ban all trade with France and restore trade with Britain. For its part, Britain agrees to stop seizing American ships. However, British foreign secretary George Canning refuses to accept the agreement and Erskine is removed from office. Both countries return to their entrenched positions, making war inevitable.

September 30. The **Treaty of Fort Wayne**, negotiated by Indiana Territory governor William Henry Harrison, procures about three million acres of Indian land for white settlers in Illinois and Indiana. The Shawnee, who were not included in the negotiations, insist the treaty is illegal. Their leader Tecumseh warns Harrison that unless the treaty is nullified, the Shawnee and the American Indian Confederation will seek an alliance with the British—it is not, and they do. The British supply weapons and ammunition via Canada and the tribes continue to harass and attack settlers and America militiamen until Tecumseh's death in 1813. British support for the Native American uprising is yet another catalyst for the war.

1810

March 23. Napoleon's **Rambouillet Decree** declares that all American ships entering a French port are to be confiscated along with their cargo and crew.

May 1. With America's economy reeling and merchant ships being seized, the United States enacts **Macon Bill No. 2**, an act introduced by Representative Nathaniel Macon to lift all embargoes with Britain and France. The bill adds that if either France or Britain continues to attack American ships, the United States will cease trading with the aggressor but continue to supply the other. The Macon Bill does not have the desired effect as *both* Britain and France continue to attack American merchant ships.

August 5. Fearing the United States might declare war on France because of the Rambouillet Decree, the Duc de Cadore writes to General

William Henry Harrison
(portrait by
Rembrandt Peale)

John Armstrong, the American ambassador to France. The **Cadore Letter,** largely dictated by Napoleon, promises to lift the Berlin and Milan decrees if the Americans will continue to ban trade with Britain. On the same day, however, France increases the tariff on a number of goods from the American colonies so that even if trade were to resume between America and France, the tax on the goods would be prohibitive. It affects twenty-one items from only the American colonies—for example, the duty on cotton rises from 60 francs to 800 francs.

1811

February 2. Because the Royal Navy continues to attack American ships, all trade with Britain is banned under the terms of Macon Bill No. 2.

March 10. The **Henry Letters** surface. They were written by John Henry, a spy and rogue commissioned in 1809 by Sir James Craig, governor-general of Canada, to gather intelligence about what was happening in the New England states. Henry was promised a high position in Canada, but the promise was never fulfilled as Craig died shortly thereafter. In revenge, Henry doctored the letters and sold them to President Madison for $50,000. The letters detail how he had been operating in Canada

Commodore John Rodgers, Captain of the
USS *President* (print of an engraving
dated 1856, artist unknown)

Commodore John Rodgers
(oil on canvas by Stuart Gilbert)

for the British government to try to persuade the New England states
to leave the United States and join Canada. Their publication further
increases tensions among America, Britain, and Canada.

May 16. A naval battle known as the *Little Belt* **Affair**, another catalyst
for war, takes place between the frigate USS *President* and the British
sloop *Little Belt*. At the beginning of May, HMS *Guerriere* stopped the
USS *Spitfire* off Sandy Hook, New Jersey, and impressed apprentice
sailing master John Diggio, a U.S. citizen. Secretary of the Navy Paul
Hamilton then ordered the *President* to patrol the waters. On May 16,
Commodore John Rodgers, captain of the *President*, spots a Royal Navy
warship that he believes to be the *Guerriere*. As Rodgers closes, however,
he realizes the ship is not the *Guerriere* but a much smaller vessel. Neither
vessel identifies itself when hailed, and cannon fire erupts. The battle is
short lived and the *Little Belt*, heavily outgunned, limps away to Halifax,
Nova Scotia. Both sides claim they were the victim, each insisting the
other side fired first.

November 4. With growing hostility toward the British, the **12th U.S.**

The USS *Constitution*'s First Victory at Sea, over HMS *Guerriere*
(oil on canvas by Anton Otto Fischer)

William Henry Harrison
(print by Albert Gallatin Hoit)

Henry Clay
(print of an engraving dated 1856, artist unknown)

Congress meets and is in the mood for war. Many of those elected won their seats campaigning for war. They are known as the War Hawks and are led by Henry Clay.

November 7. While Congress is still in session, Governor Harrison of the Indiana Territory and his militia are attacked by Tecumseh's American Indian Confederation forces, led by Tecumseh's younger brother, Tenskwatawa, at the **Battle of Tippecanoe**. The Indians are quickly defeated. It is widely believed—and later proved—that the British were supporting the uprising. War with Britain will break out just six months later.

The Battle of Tippecanoe
(print of an engraving by artist Alonzo Chappel)

TWO

THE BIRTH OF THE NAVY

I F THE NEW CONSTITUTION is adopted, as there is reason to expect," John Paul Jones wrote in December 1787, "America will soon be a very respectable Nation; and the creation of a Marine Force will necessarily be among the first objects of her policy."[5] The Constitutional Convention in 1787 proposed giving Congress power to raise money to "provide and maintain a navy." While the Constitution restricted army appropriations to two years, it left the term of naval appropriations unlimited. As Thomas Jefferson observed, "A naval force can never endanger our liberties, nor occasion bloodshed; a land force would do both."

However, at the time of Jones's death in 1792, the Revenue Cutter Service, a forerunner to the Coast Guard, was the only naval force. The following year, British warships started to harass American merchant vessels trading with France. American vessels were also being attacked in the Mediterranean and Atlantic approaches. Corsairs from the Barbary Coast ports of Morocco, Algiers, Tripoli, and Tunis had for decades attacked foreign vessels unless a tribute was paid. Before the American Revolution, American ships were protected from these pirates by the British Royal Navy, which had several squadrons stationed in the Mediterranean. After the Revolution, of course, America had lost this protection. In 1785, corsairs had captured two American merchant ships holding the crew and twenty-two passengers for ransom. Many of the prisoners remained in captivity for more than a decade.

Various countries patrolled the western Mediterranean to try to control the corsairs. Their actions restricted the pirates' activities largely

---

5. Crawford and Hughes, *The Reestablishment of the Navy*, 3.

Captain John Paul Jones
(portrait by Cecilia Beaux)

Henry Knox
(portrait by Gilbert Stuart)

to the Barbary Coast. However, in 1793, Portugal signed a treaty with the Algerine corsairs that allowed them to sail into the Atlantic to attack foreign vessels. By the end of that year, more than a hundred Americans were being held by the pirates.

On January 2, 1794, the House of Representatives agreed that "a naval force adequate to the protection of the commerce of the United States, against the Algerine corsairs, ought to be provided." On January 20, a committee set up to determine the size of this naval force proposed the building of six frigates. There was still considerable opposition within Congress, but this was overcome when Britain unilaterally prohibited all foreign ships from trading with the French West Indies and dispatched its fleet to enforce the measure. An act was then passed by Congress "to provide a naval armament in the form of six frigates, four of forty-four guns each and two of thirty-six, by purchase or otherwise." The bill was signed into law by President George Washington on March 27, 1794, although it would take almost four more years before the first three frigates were commissioned.

America had signed a treaty with Morocco for safe passage of its ships in 1786. However, it could not secure a deal with Algeria until 1795, when it agreed to pay a ransom of more than $1 million—one-sixth of

Argus Burning British Vessels (print by Abel Bowen)

the entire American budget—for the release of the 115 American sailors being held. Algeria's insistence on further payments to prevent attacks on other American ships finally persuaded the Americans to act and build the warships that were so desperately needed.

Henry Knox, the secretary of war, was tasked with building the frigates. The passing of the act, he said, "created an anxious solicitude that this second commencement of a navy for the United States should be worthy of their national character. That the vessels should combine such qualities of strength, durability, swiftness of sailing, and force, as to render them equal, if not superior, to any frigates belonging to any of the European Powers." The six frigates were the *Constitution* (commissioned in 1797), the *Constellation* (1797), the *United States* (1797), the *Congress* (1799), the *Chesapeake* (1800), and the *President* (1800).

Despite financial and political obstacles, Benjamin Stoddert, the first secretary of the navy, was determined to build a navy capable of protecting the nation's vital trading interests. He established six navy yards. In a December 1798 proposal to Congress, he advocated building twelve ships of the line, twelve frigates, and twenty ships of up to twenty-four guns.

Congress agreed to build the twelve frigates, but in 1801, incoming President Thomas Jefferson insisted on further reducing the navy's budget. At the same time, the pasha of Tripoli demanded $225,000 from the U.S. administration as tribute for not interfering with American vessels. Jefferson refused, and on May 10, 1801, the pasha declared war on the United States.

In 1802, Congress passed "an Act for the Protection of Commerce and seamen of the United States against the Tripolitan cruisers," empowering the president to use what force was necessary to protect American

Decatur Boarding the Tripolitan Gunboat
(oil by Dennis Malone Carter)

interests, vessels, and lives. The USS *Argus*, *Chesapeake*, *Constellation*, *Constitution*, *Enterprise*, *Intrepid*, *Philadelphia*, and *Syren* all saw action during the First Barbary War, which lasted four years. The two most significant battles were the Battle of Tripoli (July 1804) and the Battle of Derna (April–May 1805). In the latter, a force led by U.S. Marine First Lieutenant Presley O'Bannon with eight Marines and about five hundred mercenaries marched across the desert from Alexandria, Egypt, to capture the port city of Derna. It was the first time that the U.S. flag was raised in victory on foreign soil. The battle is memorialized in the "Marines' Hymn" with the line "to the shores of Tripoli."

Burning of the Frigate *Philadelphia* in the Harbor of Tripoli
(oil on canvas by Edward Moran)

George Brown,
Boatswain's Mate,
U.S. Navy
(print by
unknown artist)

A peace treaty between the United States and Tripoli was signed on June 10, 1805. It required both parties to return what prisoners they held, and the United States to pay a sum of $60,000, since it held fewer prisoners. But the peace was short lived. By 1807, Algerian pirates were again capturing American vessels and holding the seamen for ransom. By this time, however, America was preoccupied with the growing conflict with Britain. (In 1815, at the end of the 1812 war, the United States did send a strong naval force to the Mediterranean, which was successful in the Second Barbary War, finally ending the practice of paying tributes.)

The outcome of the First Barbary War and the escalating dispute with Britain convinced both the president and Congress that America needed a strong navy to protect its commerce and its merchant fleet on the high seas.

WASHINGTON NAVY YARD

The Washington Navy Yard is the U.S. Navy's oldest shore establishment, in operation since the first decade of the nineteenth century. It evolved from a shipbuilding center to ordnance plant and then to the ceremonial and administrative center for the navy. Today, the yard is home to the chief of naval operations and headquarters for the Naval Historical Center and numerous naval commands.

The land was purchased under an act of July 23, 1798, with two additional lots being purchased in 1801. The Washington Navy Yard was

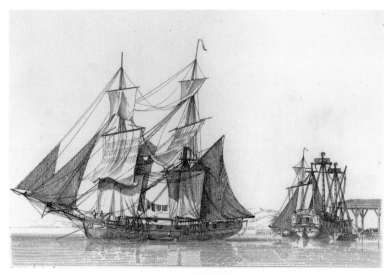

A U.S. Merchant Brig Drying Her Sails While at Anchor
(print by Jean Jerome Baugean)

established on October 2, 1799, the date the property was transferred to the navy. The yard was built under the direction of Secretary Stoddert under the supervision of the yard's first commandant, Commodore Thomas Tingey, who would serve in that capacity for twenty-nine years.

The original boundaries that were established in 1800, along 9th and M Streets, SE, are still marked by a white brick wall that surrounds the navy yard on the north and east sides. The north wall of the yard was built in 1809 along with a guardhouse. After the fire of 1814, Commodore Tingey recommended that the height of the eastern wall be increased to ten feet, since, along with the fire, looting by the local populace took its toll.

The southern boundary of the yard was formed by the Anacostia River, then called the Eastern Branch of the Potomac River. The west side was undeveloped marshland. The land along the Anacostia was added to by landfill over the years as it became necessary to reclaim additional land for the navy yard.

The first years saw the Washington Navy Yard become the navy's largest shipbuilding and shipfitting facility, with twenty-two vessels constructed there, ranging from small 70-foot gunboats to the 246-foot steam frigate *Minnesota*. The USS *Constitution* came to the yard in 1812 to refit and prepare for combat action. Robert Fulton conducted research and testing on his clockwork torpedo there during the War of 1812.

The Washington Navy Yard was a vital support facility and a strategic link in the defense of the capital. As the British marched into Washington, holding the yard became impossible. Commodore Tingey,

USS *Constitution* Battles HMS *Java*
(oil on canvas by Charles Robert Patterson)

seeing the smoke from the burning Capitol, ordered the yard burned to prevent its capture by the enemy.[6] Tingey's own quarters (now Quarters A) and the Latrobe Gate were spared the flames.[7]

CONSTRUCTION OF THE FIRST SIX FRIGATES

As the Department of the Navy had not yet been created, the task of building the six frigates fell to three successive secretaries of war—Henry Knox (1794–1795), Timothy Pickering (1795–1796), and James McHenry (1796–1798). The original proposal was to buy suitable merchant ships and convert them, but after lengthy discussions with naval architects and navy captains, the administration agreed to build new vessels. On April 15, 1794, Knox recommended the construction of six new frigates that would be superior in every way to any similar vessel in any European navy.

> To keep labor costs down, government employees rather than private contractors would build the ships, and construction sites would be distributed geographically in order to spread the economic benefit and win popular support. "It is just and wise to proportion . . . benefits as nearly as may be to those places or states which pay the greatest amount to its support," Knox advised. Although it might be cheaper to build the frigates successively in a single place, "a few thousand dollars in the expences will be no object compared with the satisfaction a just distribution would afford."[8]

President Washington approved six construction sites: Portsmouth, New Hampshire; Boston; New York; Philadelphia; Baltimore; and Gosport (Norfolk), Virginia.

---

6. Following the War of 1812, the Washington Navy Yard never regained its prominence in shipbuilding activity. The waters of the Anacostia River were too shallow to accommodate larger vessels, and the yard was deemed too inaccessible to the open sea. The yard's focus changed to ordnance and technology. The fourteen-inch naval railway guns used in France during World War I were manufactured at the yard, and by World War II the yard was the largest naval ordnance plant in the world. Weapons designed and built there were used in every war in which the United States fought until the 1960s.

7. This section is reproduced from the U.S. Naval History and Heritage Command's "History of the Washington Navy Yard," http://www.history.navy.mil/faqs/faq52-1.htm.

8. Crawford and Hughes, *Reestablishment of the Navy*, 6.

At each site, a civilian naval constructor was hired to direct the work. Navy captains were appointed as superintendents, one for each of the six frigates. John Barry, last officer of the Continental Navy in active service, received commission number one as the first officer in the new United States Navy.[9]

TABLE 2.1

Site	Frigate	Guns	Superintendent	Naval Constructor
Portsmouth	Congress	36	James Sever	James Hackett
Boston	Constitution	44	Samuel Nicholson	George Claghorn
New York	President	44	Silas Talbot	Forman Cheeseman
Philadelphia	United States	44	John Barry	Joshua Humphreys
Baltimore	Constellation	36	Thomas Truxtun	David Stodder
Gosport	Chesapeake	36	Richard Dale	Josiah Fox

In March 1795, Pickering prepared a list of ten suggested names for the ships, and Washington is reported to have chosen five—*Constitution, United States, President, Constellation,* and *Congress.* The *Chesapeake* was not named until sometime later.

Supplies were difficult to come by and construction was slow. The main frames of the ships were constructed from live oak that had to be transported up from the forests in the South. The ships were still in the early stages of construction in early 1796 when news was received of the peace treaty with Algiers. Although the act authorizing the frigates stipulated that construction should be halted if a peace deal was reached, Washington urged Congress to complete the frigates. Congress approved the completion of three of the ships—*United States, Constellation,* and *Constitution.* The other three were mothballed. The *United States* was launched in Philadelphia on May 10, 1797; the *Constellation* in Baltimore on September 7, 1797; and the *Constitution* in Boston on October 21, 1797.

Addressing Congress in December 1796, Washington urged the "gradual creation of a navy" for the protection of the country's commerce, but Congress refused to authorize completion of the remaining three frigates. The legislators changed their minds in July 1797, though, when the revolutionary government in France declared that American ships trading with Britain—under a commercial agreement signed in 1794—breached

---

9. Crawford and Hughes, *Reestablishment of the Navy,* 6.

USS *Chesapeake*
(oil on canvas by Frank Muller)

John Adams
(portrait by
Asher B. Durand)

a 1774 trading treaty between the United States and France. When the French increased their seizures of American merchant ships, cargoes, and crews, Congress authorized President John Adams to have the remaining three frigates built and put to sea as quickly as possible. In December 1797, Adams told Congress that the French refused to negotiate and that America had "to place our country in a suitable posture of defense."

In April of 1798, President Adams informed Congress of the infamous "XYZ Affair," in which three French agents demanded a large bribe for the restoration of relations with the United States. Outraged by this affront to national honor, on April 27, 1798, Congress authorized the President to acquire, arm, and man no more than twelve vessels, of up to twenty-two guns each. Under the terms of this act several vessels were purchased and converted into ships of war. One of these, the *Ganges*, a Philadelphia-built merchant ship, became "the first man-of-war to fit out and get to sea—on May 24, 1798—under the second organization of the Navy."[10]

---

10. Crawford and Hughes, *Reestablishment of the Navy*, 7–8, quoting U.S. Naval History Division, *Dictionary of American Naval Fighting Ships*, edited by James L. Mooney et al. (Washington, DC: Government Printing Office, 1959-1981), 3:17.

Secretary McHenry told Congress that responsibility for naval affairs was taking up too much of his and his department's time. As a result, on April 30, 1798, President Adams signed an act creating the Department of the Navy. Benjamin Stoddert was appointed its first secretary.

On May 28, Congress gave authorization for U.S. vessels to capture any armed French vessel off the U.S. coast, thus starting the undeclared Quasi-War with France.

That conflict led to the rapid passage of several pieces of naval legislation. An act of June 30 gave the President authority to accept ships on loan from private citizens, who would be paid in interest-bearing government bonds. On July 9, Congress authorized U.S. naval vessels to capture armed French vessels anywhere on the high seas, not just off the coast of the United States. This act also sanctioned the issuance of privateering commissions. Two days later, the President signed the act that established the United States Marine Corps. On July 16, Congress appropriated funds to build and equip the three remaining frigates begun under the Act of 1794: *Congress*, launched at Portsmouth, N.H., on August 15, 1799; *Chesapeake*, at Gosport, Va., on December 2, 1799; and *President*, at New York, N.Y., on April 10, 1800.[11]

The fledgling U.S. Navy had been launched.

USS *Constitution*: "OLD IRONSIDES"

Authorized by Congress in 1794, built in 1797, and launched in 1798, the USS *Constitution* saw action in one undeclared war and two official wars and had a perfect battle record—never beaten in battle or boarded.[12] She also became synonymous with the power that was the emerging U.S. Navy.

Her first action was in the Quasi-War, protecting American merchant ships against French attack in the Atlantic and West Indies. When the war ended in 1801, the *Constitution* sailed to the Mediterranean to protect American ships from attack off the Barbary Coast. Jefferson refused to pay the Barbary States a tribute to ensure the safe passage of American vessels and instead sent a naval squadron, including the *Constitution*, to

11. Crawford and Hughes, *Reestablishment of the Navy*, 8.

12. U.S. Naval History and Heritage Command, *Old Ironsides' Battle Record: Documents of USS* Constitution's *Illustrious Deeds*, http://www.history.navy.mil/docs/war1812/consti.htm.

Sailing Master in Full Dress
Uniform, War of 1812
(watercolor by Lieutenant Rex
Cressman Reichart)

Enlisted Member of Barge Crew in
Typical Dress Uniform,
War of 1812 (watercolor by Lieutenant
Rex Cressman Reichart)

Captain in Full Dress Uniform,
War of 1812 (watercolor by Lieutenant
Rex Cressman Reichart)

protect America's maritime and trading interests. The *Constitution* was on station for four years and took part in the bombardment of Tripoli in August 1804.

For the next eight years, the USS *Constitution* helped patrol the western Atlantic and West Indies, protecting American merchant ships from being seized by British warships. In 1812, when the United States declared war on Britain, the *Constitution* took part in several engagements with Britain, earning the nickname "Old Ironsides" because of her apparent invincibility. Because of her size and overwhelming firepower, the Royal Navy ordered its captains to stop the practice of one-on-one battles with U.S. warships.

When war was declared, the *Constitution* had just left Alexandria, Virginia, for Annapolis, Maryland, and after resupplying she set sail for New York. Unknown to her captain, Isaac Hull, a squadron of British warships was assembling off New York to blockade the harbor. On July 15, the *Constitution* ran into HMS *Guerriere*, which was soon joined by four other vessels in pursuit of the American warship.[13]

---

13. U.S. Naval History and Heritage Command, "Escape from an Enemy Squadron, 1812," *Old Ironsides' Battle Record*, http://www.history.navy.mil/docs/war1812/const4.htm.

Bombardment of Tripoli, August 3, 1804
(oil by M. F. Corne)

Constitution's Escape from the British
(print by M. Corne, engraving by W. Hoogland)

USS *Constitution* Being Chased by the British Fleet
(oil on canvas by Frank Muller)

Captain Hull's official report to the secretary of the navy outlines the three-day chase off the coast of New Jersey. He describes how he successfully outmaneuvered and outran the British squadron in one of the most dramatic American naval episodes. Eventually, Hull was able to dock the *Constitution* at Boston.

Captain Isaac Hull to Secretary of the Navy Paul Hamilton
U.S. Frigate Constitution
At Sea, July 21st 1812

We left Annapolis on July 5 but a strong southerly current prevented us from sailing north as planned. On the 17th, while off Egg Harbor, we spotted four warships inshore. They were too far away for us to make out whether

USS *Constitution* Escaping the British Fleet
(oil on copper by J. Font)

they were British ships or part of the American squadron that had been trapped in New York and had managed to break out.

At four in the afternoon we sighted another ship under full sail and gave chase, hoping that when dark fell we would be able to see her signals and know whether she was an enemy ship or not. At 10 in the evening, the ship was about six miles away and we saw her signaling to the other ships close to the shore. Realizing that all five ships were the enemy's, we made off under full sail, and then laid off until daylight to see what was happening.

On the 18th at daylight, we saw the enemy ships heading towards us. We were becalmed so we lowered the boats to tow us. The enemy frigates,

USS *Constitution* Kedging to Escape the British Fleet
(oil on board by Frank Ochs)

about five miles behind, did the same. Having the advantage of a light
breeze, they were catching up fast.

I ordered several guns moved to the stern and cleared the ship for
action. At about seven in the morning, I ordered one of the guns to fire at
the nearest frigate in the hopes of disabling her masts, but the shot fell short.

At 8am the enemy ships, having six or eight boats ahead towing
each of them, were getting closer and I realized we would have no chance
against four heavily armed frigates if they caught up with us. I dispatched
two anchors with four hundred fathoms of rope in the boats. The boats
rowed ahead of us and then dropped the anchors and we used them to haul
ourselves forward. We began to pull ahead of the enemy, but they adopted
the same plan. Around 9am the nearest enemy ship opened fire with her

Chase of the *Constitution*
(painting by Anton Otto Fischer)

The Crew of the *Constitution* Towing the Warship in Their Longboats
(print by Carlton T. Chapman)

bow guns. *Their shots fell short, but I am sure that some of our stern shots hit the enemy as we did not see them hit the water.*

Soon after 9am a second frigate fired a broadside, but again her shots fell short. For the next three hours all hands were employed in trying to keep ahead of the enemy. About two in the afternoon, all the boats pulling the enemy ships were sent to the leading frigate. But by that time a light breeze had sprung up and with our boats still towing us we were able to keep out of range of the enemy guns even though their frigates came very close to us. Around 11pm the breeze picked up and we were able to bring the boats aboard and keep ahead of the enemy.

Around dawn on the 19th we were within gunshot of one of the frigates, but it did not fire on us for fear of becoming becalmed as the wind was light. At this time we could see six enemy ships chasing us.

At 9 we spotted an American merchant ship. The enemy ships all hoisted American colors in the hopes of drawing her to them. I hoisted English colors and the merchant ship made good her escape.

The wind gradually increased all day and we managed to pull six to eight miles ahead of the enemy, but they continued to give chase.

At dawn on the 20th we could only spot three of the enemy ships, the closest about 12 miles away. We wetted the sails to give us extra speed and

Captain Isaac Hull
(oil on canvas by
Samuel L. Waldo)

soon left the enemy far behind. They gave up the chase, changed course, and headed for station off New York. A short time later we spotted an American brig bound for Portland and I directed the captain what course to steer to avoid the enemy. A second American brig for Philadelphia was similarly warned and decided to sail for Charleston instead.

With the enemy ships stationed off New York, I determined to make for Boston to receive further orders.

This confrontation with the enemy and the subsequent chase is the reason your previous orders were not carried out.

I cannot close without expressing to you the confidence I have in the brave officers and crew under my command. Their conduct while under the guns of the enemy was such as might have been expected from American officers and seamen.

Isaac Hull[14]

---

14. National Archives, Record Group 45, Captain's Letters, 1812, Vol. 2, No. 127.

THREE

Declaration of War

O N JUNE 1, 1812, President James Madison addressed Congress citing a long list of America's grievances against Great Britain. The House of Representatives voted to declare war (79–49) and the Senate followed with a 19–13 vote in favor. Madison signed the measure into law on June 18, 1812, and America was officially at war with Britain.

However, many opposed the war in America, and not a single Federalist in Congress voted to support it. Riots took place in many parts of the country, both for and against the war. In Baltimore, a group of Federalists was attacked and accused of near treason for their opposition to the war. Many others opposed the war on religious grounds.

The First Year, 1812

Five days after America declared war, the British government formally repealed its Orders in Council in a bid to placate the Americans. The ship sailing from America with the news that the United States was at war with Britain presumably passed the vessel from Britain carrying news of the Orders in Council's repeal. However, it was many days more before each side learned what the other had done.

On June 24, a courier informed British government representatives in Montreal about the declaration of war, and on June 28 the message was relayed to British military commanders in the field and Royal Navy captains in the area.

Fort Mackinac, Michigan
(oil on canvas by Seth Eastman)

The following day, two schooners, the *Sophia* and *Island Packet*, were seized by Canadian partisans and burned. The schooners were part of a convoy of eight anchored in Ogdensburg on the St. Lawrence River that tried to break out into Lake Ontario. The other six ships returned to Ogdensburg. America retaliated on July 1 by doubling customs duties on all goods entering U.S. ports.

On July 12, William Hull, governor of the Michigan Territory and a recently appointed brigadier general in charge of the new Army of the Northwest, marched his men across the border to Sandwich (now Windsor) in Upper Canada on what would be a short-lived invasion. His men were attacked by Canadian and Native American forces loyal to Britain. On July 16, an American patrol under the command of Colonel Lewis Cass was sent out to see how close it could get to Amherstburg.

The patrol ran into two British soldiers, James Hancock and John Dean, defending the bridge over the Canard River. In the ensuing skirmish, Hancock was killed and Dean was taken prisoner. Hancock became the first British casualty of the war. Although Cass captured the bridge, he never received supplies and had to withdraw to Sandwich. The following day, Hull learned that Fort Mackinac had been captured by the British, and he marched his army back across the border.

Fort Mackinac was built on Mackinac Island by the British during the Revolutionary War but handed over to the United States in 1796. A small force of sixty men under the command of Lieutenant Porter Hanks guarded the U.S. garrison. On the morning of July 17, they were attacked by about two hundred British troops and a force of several hundred Native Americans in bateaux[15] and war canoes. Hanks surrendered without a fight. He and his men were set free after promising not to take up arms again. The British then built a much more substantial stockade, Fort George, on the highest point on the island.[16]

On July 19, five British warships attacked a U.S. naval shipyard at Sackets Harbor, New York. Because of its strategic position on Lake Ontario, the shipyard had been heavily fortified and thousands of troops were billeted in the village. In the harbor was the sixteen-gun brig USS *Oneida* with her prize the *Lord Nelson*, a British schooner that had been captured on June 5. The *Oneida* was unable to escape, so all her cannons were moved to protect the harbor entrance. The firepower from her guns and the shore battery forced the British ships to break off the action after a two-hour battle.

The Battle of Brownstown, south of Fort Detroit, demonstrated how unprepared the untrained American militia was. On August 5, a force of two hundred that had been sent to escort a supply train were set upon by a band of Indians—numbering no more than twenty-five—and a handful of British troops commanded by Major Adam Muir, who was in charge of the regiment at Amherstburg. The militia fled, with eighteen men killed, twelve wounded, and seventy missing. Only half of the force made it back to Fort Detroit. The other side suffered almost no casualties.

---

15. Flat-bottomed boats.

16. Lieutenant Hanks made his way back to Detroit, where he was charged with cowardice. While waiting for his court-martial, the British attacked Fort Detroit and he was decapitated by a cannonball.

On August 6, British Major General Isaac Brock sailed with a small unit of regulars and volunteers from the York militia to reinforce the garrison at Amherstburg, which faced General Hull's position across Lake Erie in Detroit. Following the Battle of Brownstown, Hull sent out a force of more than six hundred regulars and volunteers under the command of Lieutenant Colonel James Miller to collect the supplies. On August 8, the Americans were confronted by Muir and his troops, supported by Canadian militiamen and Native Americans, and a brief, chaotic battle ensued. At one point, the British thought they were being attacked from the flanks and opened fire on their own Indian allies. The British retreated in confusion until Muir rallied his troops and set up another battle line. Miller was able to advance, but was reluctant to engage the British again. Claiming the advance as a victory, he marched his men home.

On August 13, the USS *Essex*, on patrol off Bermuda, captured HMS *Alert* after a brief engagement. By the time she returned to New York in September, she had taken ten British ships as prizes.

On August 15, Fort Dearborn, in what is now Chicago, was being evacuated on the orders of Hull. Captain Nathan Heald was leading sixty-six U.S. regulars and militia away from the fort, along with nine women and eighteen children, when they were ambushed by a band of Potawatomi Indians. In the brief battle, twenty-six regulars, twelve militia, two women, and twelve children were killed and all the rest were taken prisoner. The Indians sold the captives to the British, who released them immediately. The fort was burned to the ground. Because women and children were killed, the battle is sometimes referred to as the Dearborn Massacre.

The war was not going well for the Americans. On August 15, the British started a bombardment of Fort Detroit, and the following day, General Brock and his troops tricked Hull into surrendering both the fort and the town.

Hull, even though his force outnumbered the British, was low on supplies. Brock arranged for a letter to fall into American hands that claimed that there were already five thousand Indians at Amherstburg ready to attack. When he was sure Hull would have seen the letter, Brock sent the American general a letter demanding the fort's surrender. He wrote, "The force at my disposal authorizes me to require of you the immediate surrender of Fort Detroit. It is far from my intention to join in a war of extermination, but you must be aware, that the numerous

Essex and *Alert*
(print by unknown artist)

body of Indians who have attached themselves to my troops, will be beyond control the moment the contest commences."[17]

Brock also used a number of other deceptions to convince Hull that he was up against a superior force. He dressed the Canadian militia in British army uniforms and ordered hundreds of campfires to be lit. Traditionally, each unit had its own bonfire, so by ordering hundreds of bonfires, it appeared there were many more units than actually existed.

On the morning of August 16, Tecumseh's warriors crossed the Detroit River, followed by Brock and about 350 soldiers. The original plan was to lay siege to the fort, but Brock decided to advance and attack the fort's weakest side. Believing himself heavily outnumbered and fearing a massacre of the women and children inside the fort, Hull raised the white flag and surrendered his entire force.

Almost six hundred American regulars were sent as prisoners to Quebec City, while the American militiamen were given safe passage out of the area. The British captured 30 cannons, 300 rifles, and 2,500 muskets, which they gave to the Canadian militia. The capture of the fort also encouraged more Indians in the region to side with the British and attack American military outposts. The British held on to Fort Detroit for just over a year. Hull was court-martialed and sentenced to death, but Madison commuted the sentence to dismissal from the army because of his honorable service in the Revolutionary War.

---

17. *The War of 1812*, extracted from American Military History, Army Historical Series, Office of the Chief of Military History, U.S. Army.

The USS *Constitution* in Action against HMS *Guerriere*
(oil on canvas by John Trumbull)

On August 19, one of the most memorable events of the war took place when the USS *Constitution*—"Old Ironsides"—captured HMS *Guerriere*.

The thirty-eight-gun *Guerriere* was built by the French, but was captured by HMS *Blanche* in July 1806. She was refitted at Chatham Dockyard east of London and commissioned into the Royal Navy.

The *Constitution*, under the command of Captain Isaac Hull, was on patrol about four hundred miles southeast of Halifax, Nova Scotia. It was only three weeks since the *Constitution* had evaded capture by a Royal Navy squadron led by the *Guerriere*, but this time the British warship was alone. The two ships closed to do battle.

Broadsides were exchanged for more than thirty minutes before the *Guerriere* lost first her mizzenmast and then her foremast and mainmast, crippling her with her main deck guns underwater. The *Constitution* closed in to rake the decks with pistol and musket fire. To avoid further loss of life, Captain James R. Dacres struck his colors and surrendered. The *Constitution* sent across a boarding party, but the British warship was too badly damaged to save. The injured were transferred to the *Constitution*, and the *Guerriere* was set on fire and sunk. Ironically, many

The Battle between the USS *Constitution* and HMS *Guerriere*
(engraving by W. Strickland)

USS *Constitution* vs. HMS *Guerriere*
(engraving by Thomas Gimbrede)

of the boarding party from *Constitution* were British seaman who had switched sides and joined the U.S. Navy. In the battle, twenty-one British crewmen were killed or died shortly after from their wounds, and fifty-seven were wounded. The Americans suffered nine dead and thirteen wounded.

The *Constitution* returned victorious to Boston. Captain Dacres was later exonerated by a court-martial, which found he was justified in surrendering his ship in order to save further loss of life. Captain Hull's official account of *Constitution*'s victory over the *Guerriere* read as follows:

Captain Isaac Hull to Secretary of the Navy Paul Hamilton
U.S. Frigate Constitution, *off Boston Light, August 28, 1812*

Sir,

On the 19th of August at about 2pm we spotted a sail, but at such a distance that we could not identify the vessel. We hoisted all sail and made chase. We quickly caught up with her and around 3.30pm we were able to identify her as a large frigate. We cleared the ship for action and gave three cheers. As we approached, the enemy vessel hoisted the English ensign and at five minutes past five, the enemy fired a broadside but her shot fell short. She then turned and fired a broadside from her larboard guns. Two shots struck us but without causing injuries. As we were within gunshot, I ordered the ensign hoisted.

At five minutes past six being alongside and within less than pistol shot range, we commended heavy fire from all our guns loaded with shot and grape. In less than 15 minutes most of the enemy's masts and sails had been so badly damaged that the ship was difficult to control. We had sustained little damage.

We turned and fired several broadsides which made great havoc amongst his men and further disabled the ship. I decided to board her but as we did so, her remaining masts fell overboard and she was totally disabled.

We sailed a little way off to make repairs. On our return to the scene, I dispatched a boat with Lieutenant Reed on board under a flag of truce to see if the enemy had surrendered and if so, what assistance was needed as I believed she was sinking.

Mr. Reed returned with James Richard Dacres, Commander of HMS Guerriere, *who surrendered his ship to the* Constitution. *We immediately*

sent more boats to bring the injured crew and their baggage aboard although this took all night. At daylight we found the Guerriere a wreck and I decided to set her on fire as it was impossible to get her into port.

At 3pm Mr. Reed was ordered to set fire to the Guerriere's store rooms and in a very short time she blew up.

I must express to you the bravery and gallant conduct of the officers and crew under my command during the action. So well directed and intense was the fire of the Constitution that in less than 30 minutes, the Guerriere was left without a spar standing and the hull cut to pieces and taking on water.

Actions like these speak for themselves which makes it unnecessary for me to say anything to establish the bravery and gallant conduct of those that were engaged in it. Were I to name any particular Officer as having been more useful than the rest, I should do them great injustice, they all fought bravely, and gave me every possible assistance that I could wish.

Isaac Hull[18]

The official British version of the battle by *Guerriere's* captain was less ecstatic.

Captain James R. Dacres, Royal Navy, to Vice Admiral Herbert Sawyer, Royal Navy
Boston, September 7, 1812

Sir,

I am sorry to inform you of the capture of HMS Guerriere by the American frigate Constitution after a severe action on August 19. At 2pm we saw a sail bearing down on us. At 3pm we identified her as a man of war and prepared for action. At 4.10 we hoisted our Colors and fired several shots at her. At 4.20 she returned fire and kept this up until 5.20 when our mizzen mast went overboard. The enemy ship was then able to rake us at will while his riflemen fired at anyone on deck. At 5.40 as the enemy prepared to board I received a severe wound in the back. We managed to break away but at 6.20 our fore and aft masts went over the

18. National Archives, Record Group 45, Captain's Letters, 1812, Vol. 2, No. 207.

side leaving us an unmanageable wreck. As we worked to clear the wreckage our main guns were under water and we were at the mercy of the enemy. I called my few remaining officers together, and they were of the opinion that any future resistance would be a needless waste of lives. Reluctantly, I ordered the Colors to be struck.

The loss of the ship can be blamed on the early fall of the mizzen mast which enabled our opponent to choose his position. I am sorry to say that we suffered severely in killed and wounded—in all 15 killed and 63 wounded, many of them severely although none of the wounded officers quitted the deck until the firing ceased.

The enemy frigate proved to be the USS Constitution *and her loss in comparison was trifling—nine killed and 13 wounded.*

The Guerriere *was so cut up that all attempts to get her into port would have been useless. As soon as the wounded were taken off, she was set on fire.*

I feel it is my duty to state that the conduct of Captain Hull and his officers to our men has been that of a brave enemy, the greatest care being taken to prevent our men losing the smallest trifle, and the greatest attention paid to the wounded.

I hope, though success has not crowned our efforts, you will not think it presumptuous of me to say that the greatest credit is due to the officers and ship's company for their exertions, particularly when exposed to the heavy raking fire of the enemy.

I hope, in considering the circumstances, you will think the ship entrusted to my charge was properly defended; the unfortunate loss of our Masts, the absence of the third lieutenant, second Lieutenant of Marines, three Midshipmen, and twenty four Men considerably weakened our crew, and we only mustered at quarters 244 Men and 19 Boys, on coming into action. The Enemy had such an advantage from his Marines and Riflemen when close and his superior sailing enabled him to choose his distance.

J. R. Dacres[19]

On August 19, a major hurricane that had cut a path of destruction through the Caribbean struck New Orleans. Much of the city was flooded as the levees broke. More important, the storm caused heavy damage to

19. British Public Record Office, Admiralty 1/502, Part 4, 541-45.

Action between U.S. Frigate *Constitution* and HMS *Guerriere*
(oil on canvas by M. F. Corne)

both the American and British navies. A British fleet approaching from
the south was scattered, while a small U.S. naval contingent stationed
off the coast suffered heavy damage and the USS *Louisiana*, a former
revenue cutter, was sunk. (A new USS *Louisiana*, a sixteen-gun sloop,
would later play a significant role in the Battle of New Orleans.)

On September 3, a war party of mainly Shawnee attacked the village
of Pigeon Roost, Indiana. Twenty-four settlers, including fifteen children,
were killed, and two children were kidnapped. The Pigeon Roost Massacre
was the first Indian attack in Indiana during the war.

On September 5, Fort Madison on the Mississippi was besieged by

Indians. The fort, the first built in Upper Mississippi, had been the target of many unsuccessful attacks by Sauk Indians, led by Black Hawk. As a result, the fortifications had been strengthened, which kept it from being overrun.

On September 6, Fort Wayne in the Indiana Territory came under siege from Potawatomi and Miami warriors led by Chief Winamac. The attackers burned the homes around the fort and attempted several times to burn down the fort itself. A relief column of 2,200 Kentucky militia from Newport Barracks led by General William Henry Harrison joined forces with eight hundred militia from Ohio on September 8 and arrived at the fort on September 12. Although they had been harassed by Indians day and night on their march to the fort, they arrived uncontested. For no apparent reason, Winamac suddenly called off the attack and took his men back across the Maumee River before Harrison arrived. On September 14, Harrison sent out two columns of troops and cavalry with orders to burn any Native American villages they found as punishment for the siege. They burned villages and crops, but all the Indians had fled.

General James Winchester took command of the fort, and General Harrison took his men out to destroy more villages. Meanwhile, a strong British force led by Major Adam Muir was advancing on Fort Wayne. The two armies of General Winchester and General Harrison met on October 2, and faced with a much superior force, Muir and his men withdrew to Canada.

On September 21, a small American force of about a hundred men, led by Captain Benjamin Forsyth, crossed the border into Ontario and attacked Gananoque, a village on the St. Lawrence River that had strategic importance as a forwarding point for supplies from Montreal to Kingston. Colonel Joel Stone, the garrison commander, was away from Gananoque when the Americans attacked. His men put up some resistance and then retreated. The Americans destroyed all the supplies and burned the depot down. When the British returned, they started work on a blockhouse to protect the supplies.

On October 7, General Winchester and his men arrived close to Fort Defiance, in northwestern Ohio, and for the next several weeks they were involved in skirmishes with British and Native American forces.

Two days later, U.S. Navy Lieutenant Jesse Elliott, who had been put in charge of constructing naval vessels in Lake Erie, captured the British brigs HMS *Caledonia* and HMS *Detroit*, which had been anchored off

Captain Jesse Elliott
(print by David Edwin)

Fort Erie on the Niagara River. The *Caledonia*, which was being used as a troopship, also had a valuable cargo of furs and was taken to Black Rock to be recommissioned as the USS *Caledonia*. The *Detroit*, formerly the USS *Adams*, which had been captured when the city of Detroit was taken by the British, was swept away downriver into range of British guns. Elliott beached the ship on Squaw Island and escaped to the American side of the river while British and American shore batteries finished off the *Detroit*.

The Battle of Queenston Heights on October 13 was the first major battle of the war and was fought near Queenston, Ontario. The Americans, anxious to gain a foothold on the Canadian side of the Niagara River before winter, tried several times to cross the river under withering attack from British artillery. Many boats were lost, but a few hundred Americans did make it across, only to be pinned down. For several hours, they came under artillery fire and repeated charges by British troops. Finally, when British reinforcements arrived, the Americans were forced to surrender.

The battle was significant because the Americans, who greatly outnumbered the British, lost because of poor planning and confusion among senior officers. Many of the troops simply refused to cross the river, fearing they would be killed by Native Americans. Several hundred others who did cross fled their positions and hid until their officers had surrendered. It was also significant because Major General Isaac Brock, lieutenant governor of Upper Canada and commander of all the troops stationed there, was killed by a musket ball while leading one of the charges. The British and Canadians lost twenty-two men, while the

Capture of HMS *Frolic* by USS *Wasp*
(print by Thomas Birch, engraving by S. Seymour)

Americans lost up to a hundred killed, eighty wounded, and more than nine hundred taken prisoner, including ninety seriously wounded and several senior officers. The American commander, General Stephen Van Rensselaer, resigned immediately after the battle.

On October 18, the USS *Wasp*, a sloop commanded by Master Commandant Jacob Jones, was on patrol in the Atlantic when the *Frolic*, a British brig, was spotted. Both vessels had been damaged in gales in the previous two days and so had lost some maneuverability. In the ensuing battle, which lasted less than thirty minutes, the Americans captured the *Frolic*, but both ships were badly damaged and were unable to make sail. As the boarding party from the *Wasp* tried to make repairs aboard the *Frolic*, the HMS *Poictiers* closed in. The *Wasp* was not able to outrun the British warship and surrendered, losing its short-lived prize as well. Jones and his crew were taken prisoner but released in an exchange shortly afterward. The *Frolic* could not be saved, but the *Wasp* was recommissioned into the Royal Navy as HMS *Peacock*.

On October 25, the frigate USS *United States*, commanded by Stephen

USS *Wasp*

Decatur, was on station near Madeira in the eastern North Atlantic when, shortly after dawn, lookouts spotted sails on the horizon. As the ships neared, the other vessel was identified as the British warship HMS *Macedonian*. The ships sailed parallel to each other, and the American gunners proved more accurate, quickly bringing down the *Macedonian*'s mizzen topmast. The *United States* was then able to move in and rake the British warship with shot. After three hours, Captain John Carden surrendered the *Macedonian*.

The two ships anchored side by side for two weeks while the prize

Stephen Decatur
(print by Gilbert Stuart, engraving
by David Edwin)

Stephen Decatur
(oil on wood by
John Wesley Jarvis)

William Henry Allen
(print of an engraving by
David Edwin)

crew under the command of Lieutenant William Henry Allen repaired the *Macedonian* so that she could make sail. On December 4, the *United States* sailed into New York harbor with her prize. Decatur was a national hero. The *Macedonian* was renamed the USS *Macedonian* and had a long and distinguished career in the U.S. Navy.[20]

The British intensified their blockades of U.S. ports during November, especially those in South Carolina and Georgia that traded with the West Indies.

The twenty-gun British sloop HMS *Royal George* was the largest warship patrolling Lake Ontario. She had been built for that purpose at the Royal Naval Dockyard in Kingston, Ontario, and launched in July 1809. On November 9, she ran into a squadron of seven American ships, commanded by Commodore Isaac Chauncey, but despite the squadron's best efforts, they could not catch the *Royal George*, which made it safely back to Kingston. The following day, Chauncey attacked Kingston, his cannon inflicting limited damage on the Royal Navy fleet stationed there.

Meanwhile, back in Illinois, American troops continued to attack Native American villages. A large force of Illinois militia and Indiana Rangers under the command of Colonel William Russell destroyed a Kickapoo village on Peoria Lake and then marched to meet up with a

---

20. The *United States* and *Macedonian* sailed from New York, but ran into a squadron of British warships. They managed to make it into New London, Connecticut, where they remained blockaded until the end of the war.

USS *United States* in Action against HMS *Macedonian*
(print by Thomas Birch, engraving by Benjamin Tanner)

USS *United States* vs. HMS *Macedonian*
(Samuel Seymour, engraving by J. J. Bartlett)

Battle between the USS *United States* and HMS *Macedonian*
(print by Alonzo Chappel)

column of Kentucky militia led by Major General Samuel Hopkins. The Kentucky troops would not engage the enemy and were forced back to Vincennes. As they retreated, the Kickapoo set fire to the prairie grass to speed their retreat.

The humiliated Hopkins dismissed all the men under his command and assembled a new army of Kentucky infantry, Rangers, and scouts. On November 11, he left Vincennes and marched north past the site of the 1811 Battle of Tippecanoe. The bodies of several of the buried American soldiers had been dug up and scalped. Hopkins had the men reburied and then started to burn all the Native American villages in his path. On November 21, an American scouting party was fired on near Wild Cat Creek and forced to retreat, leaving behind the body of a soldier named Dunn.

On November 22, a force of about sixty Rangers was sent to recover Dunn's body. Spotting a lone Indian on a horse, they gave chase as he led them into a narrow canyon and an ambush. Within minutes, most of the officers had been killed—easy targets because their uniforms stood out—and the rest of the Rangers fled. The incident is known as both the Battle of Wild Cat Creek and Spur's Defeat, because the Rangers used their spurs on their horses to gallop faster out of danger. Shortly after this, there were severe snowstorms, and General Hopkins marched his men back to Fort Knox and then resigned.

View of the Port of Buffalo on Lake Erie
(print of an engraving by Gavin & Duthie)

By November 23, the Americans had pulled back all their forces from eastern Canada. Their commanders now focused on Fort Erie across the Niagara River from Buffalo, New York. The original fort was closer to the river, while a new fort that commanded higher ground was still under construction when war broke out.

Brigadier General Alexander Smyth had three thousand troops under his command assembled in Buffalo—more than enough, he thought, to invade Canada. On November 27, he sent two advance forces, one to take out the gun batteries beside Fort Erie and the other to destroy the bridge over Frenchman's Creek, which the British would have to use to send in reinforcements. The gun batteries were put out of action, but some of the men, including their leader Captain William King, were unable to get back across the river and were captured the next day. Following a brief engagement with the enemy on November 28—the Battle of Frenchman's Creek—the Americans were able to only partially destroy the bridge because they withdrew after hearing that British troops from Fort Erie were advancing on them.

When Smyth got the news that the British guns had been spiked, he said, "Canada is ours. This will be a glorious day for the United States." Smyth ordered a full invasion, but a shortage of boats and too much equipment and artillery meant he could carry only about a third of his men. He decided to postpone the invasion. He tried again before dawn on November 31, but only half his men had boarded by sunup, and he

USS *Constitution* Devastates HMS *Java*
(print of a colored engraving by Nicholas Pocock)

refused to cross the river in daylight at the mercy of British riflemen. Army commanders decided the army should cease offensives and set up winter quarters. Smyth slipped away to his estate in Virginia and took no further part in the war.

William Eustis, the secretary of war, was heavily criticized because of the lack of military success and resigned in December. He was replaced by James Monroe, whose success at the post would help him become the fifth president of the United States in 1816. He was inaugurated on March 4, 1817.

The Battle of the Mississinewa on December 18 was the first American victory of the war. General Harrison was still pursuing reprisal attacks against Native American villages and ordered an expeditionary force of six hundred mounted troops, led by Colonel John Campbell, to destroy Miami villages along the Mississinewa River. Many villages were destroyed, and hundreds of Indians were killed or taken prisoner. Despite bitterly cold weather, and with many of his men suffering from frostbite, Campbell was considering returning to Fort Greenville when his force was attacked by a strong force of Native Americans. A cavalry charge finally won the day. One of the prisoners told Campbell that Tecumseh was nearby with hundreds of warriors, so Campbell headed back for Fort Greenville. It took ten days to make the journey, by which time more than three hundred of his troops were unfit for duty because of frostbite.

In December, the Royal Navy stepped up its blockade of U.S. ports, trying to seal off Chesapeake Bay and Delaware Bay. Thousands of miles farther south, there was also a lot of naval action going on. The USS *Constitution* had been sent to patrol the South Atlantic off the coast of Brazil. On the morning of December 29, lookouts spotted sails on the horizon and Captain William Bainbridge ordered the ship to sail closer. The other ship was identified as HMS *Java*, a British frigate. Both ships prepared for action.

The documents that follow are the American and English reports back to their respective navies. Captain Bainbridge writes the American dispatch, but the British account is written by the first lieutenant of the *Java*, Henry Chads. The *Java*'s defeat, the second frigate lost to the *Constitution* in six months, motivated a change in the tactics of the Royal Navy. No longer would their frigates be allowed to engage American frigates like *Constitution* alone. Only British ships of the line or squadrons were permitted to come close enough to these ships to attack.

USS *Constitution* vs. HMS *Java*
(oil on canvas by Anton Otto Fischer)

Action between U.S. Frigate *Constitution* and HMS *Java*
(oil by Charles Robert Patterson)

Journal[21] *of Commodore William Bainbridge*
Tuesday 29th December 1812

    *At 9am we discovered two strange sails. At 10am one of them headed
for land and the other steered towards us. At 11am we signaled the other
ship but it did not answer so we hoisted all sails and made off, trying to
draw the other vessel away from the neutral coast. Just after noon on the
30th, the other ship hoisted the English ensign so we took in the sails, tacked
the ship and stood by for action.*

    *At 1.50pm the enemy bore down on us, and when the other vessel was
half a mile away I gave the order to open fire. The enemy returned fire but
kept his distance. Our wheelhouse was shot away, but by 4pm the guns of
the* Constitution *had shot away all the enemy's masts and rigging and the
enemy was no longer returning fire. I moved away to make repairs and
at 5.25 returned and got very close to the enemy lying like a log upon the
water. I was about to rake his decks when he most prudently surrendered.*

---

21. During this period British ship captains entered their official reports in the
"captain's journal" (later to become the ship's log) and these were periodically forwarded
to H.M. Admiralty.

A boarding party was sent aboard to claim her as a prize and we learned that the frigate was HMS Java. Her Captain Henry Lambert was too dangerously wounded to be removed immediately, but his first officer, Lieutenant Henry Chads, returned with the boarding party to surrender. Also on board was Lt. General Thomas Hislop, appointed to Command in the East Indies. His staff officers Major Walker and Captain Wood and several other senior naval officers were destined for ships in the East Indies.

The crew and injured were brought aboard and the Java then blew up after being set on fire. The Java had 83 wounded and 57 killed.[22]

Lieutenant Henry D. Chads, Royal Navy, to Secretary of the Admiralty John W. Croker
United States Frigate Constitution *off St Salvador Dec.31st 1812*

Sir

It is with deep regret that I write that His Majesty's Ship Java *is no more, after sustaining an action on the 29th for several hours with the American Frigate* Constitution *which resulted in the capture and ultimate destruction of His Majesty's Ship. Captain Lambert being dangerously wounded in the height of the action, the melancholy task of writing the details falls on me.*

On the morning of the 29th, off the coast of Brazil, we spotted a sail and made chase. We soon made her out to be a large frigate and at noon we prepared for action. At 2.10pm the enemy fired the first broadside and we maneuvered to get the best position. The enemy continued to fire high to disable our masts and succeeded so well that we did not have full control of the ship. The enemy's raking fire was so intense that Captain Lambert ordered the ship to sail away but at that moment our foremast was shot away and this move was not possible. Shortly afterwards the main topmast went, leaving us totally unmanageable.

At 3.30 our gallant Captain received a dangerous wound in his breast and was carried below. Many of our guns could not be fired and our mizzen mast was shot away. Both ships engaged each other until 4.35 when our opponent sailed out of gunshot to make repairs for an hour leaving us an unmanageable wreck. Every effort was made by us during this time to

---

22. National Archives, Record Group 45, Captain's Letters, 1813, Vol. 1, No. 8 1/2.

repair the ship and we succeeded in clearing the masts and rigging from our guns but the heavy rolling of the ship caused our main mast to fall over the side. The enemy returned and looked set to fire so I called together the officers who agreed that having a great part of our crew killed and wounded, we would not be justified in wasting more lives. Under these circumstances, and reluctantly, our colors were lowered and we were taken possession of a little after six.

The wounded were removed to the Constitution *and Commodore Bainbridge ordered the* Java *to be set on fire. We had the satisfaction of seeing her burn rather than fall into enemy hands.*

I cannot conclude without expressing my grateful acknowledgement for the generous treatment Captain Lambert and his Officers experienced from our Gallant Enemy Commodore Bainbridge and his Officers. W H D Chads, 1st Lieut. [23]

On December 29, Paul Hamilton resigned as secretary of the navy and was replaced the following month by William Jones. Despite the navy's successes, Hamilton constantly had to fight Congress for more funding. Jones had the advantage of serving for much of the time as both secretary of the navy and secretary of the treasury.

---

23. British Public Record Office, Admiralty 1/5435.

FOUR

1813

THE BRITISH and their Native American allies were active in the northern Michigan Territory, but American forces were anxious to retake Detroit and the surrounding areas. On January 18, a large force of American troops attacked a small British unit camped across the frozen Maumee River. The engagement lasted several hours before the British finally retreated. The Americans reclaimed Frenchtown (now Monroe) on the Raisin River, about twenty-five miles south of Detroit. This was the First Battle of Frenchtown, also called the First Battle of the River Raisin.

Four days later, the British counterattacked just before dawn, surprising the untrained and unprepared American soldiers. The British captured the American commander, General James Winchester, and many American soldiers were killed by the Native Americans as they tried to surrender or escape. The Kentucky Rifle Regiment put up a gallant defense—and did beat back several waves of British attacks—but they were low on ammunition. Eventually Winchester ordered all troops in the town to surrender, having been promised by the British commander, Brigadier General Henry Procter, that they would be treated as prisoners of war.

American prisoners who were able to walk were marched north to Fort Malden. The injured remained in Frenchtown, and Procter sent for sledges to transport them. On January 23, Native Americans attacked the wounded and set fire to the buildings they were in. Almost all the wounded were killed by the fire or trying to escape it. Only a handful

Hornet Sinking the *Peacock* (print by M. Corne, engraving by Abel Bowen)

got away. News of the River Raisin Massacre angered the nation and prompted many more Americans to volunteer.[24]

The British, fearing attack from an advancing column led by General Harrison, withdrew to Brownstown, but Harrison decided the weather was too harsh to continue his attack, so he abandoned his winter campaign to retake Detroit.

On February 5, John Armstrong was named secretary of war. He was not popular, and his confirmation in the Senate barely passed—eighteen votes to fifteen. Prior to his appointment, he had been a brigadier general in charge of the port of New York's defenses.

The day before, a small squad of British troops from Prescott, Ontario, had crossed the frozen St. Lawrence River to Ogdensburg,

---

24. Nine counties in Kentucky were later named after officers who fought in the Battle of Frenchtown: Lieutenant Colonel John Allen, Major Bland Ballard, Captain John Edmonson, Major Benjamin Graves, Captain Nathaniel Hart, Captain Paschal Hickman, Captain Virgil McCracken, Captain James Meade, and Captain John Simpson.

USS *Hornet* Sinking HMS *Peacock* (engraving on steel by Abel Bowen)

Hornet and *Peacock* (print of an engraving by unknown artist)

New York, and snatched a handful of prisoners who were taken back to Canada and held in the jail at Elizabethtown. On February 6, Major Benjamin Forsyth of the Rifle Regiment led a column of two hundred men along the river from Ogdensburg to Morristown. On the morning of February 7, they crossed the river and took Elizabethtown by surprise. The Americans were freed and fifty-two British prisoners were taken.

Lieutenant Colonel "Red George" MacDonnell was in charge of the British troops in Prescott. He decided that Ogdensburg had to be taken. The Battle of Ogdensburg took place on February 22. MacDonnell's men,

Commodore David Porter
(print by Joseph Wood, engraving by David Edwin)

David Porter
(oil by John Trumbull)

backed by artillery, attacked the fort and eventually overwhelmed it. The Americans abandoned both the fort and the town. Having captured stores and munitions and burned the Americans' boats, the British withdrew and the Americans decided not to send in more troops for the duration of the war.

On February 24, the USS *Hornet* and the Royal Navy sloop HMS *Peacock* exchanged broadsides at the mouth of the Demerara River, Guyana. Again, the American gunners proved their skill and caused serious damage to the *Peacock*'s hull. The American ship was then able to rake the *Peacock* with fire, and she surrendered. The American boarding party was unable to stop water from coming in, however, and the *Peacock* sank within minutes.[25]

The battle illustrated the enormous seagoing range of the two navies as they tried to protect their own merchant ships and trading routes and inflict as much damage on the other side as possible. On March 14, the USS *Essex*, commanded by Commodore David Porter, rounded Cape

25. The USS *Wasp*, which had been captured by the British in October 1812, was renamed HMS *Peacock* in 1813 after the loss of this earlier *Peacock*. She was lost in a storm the following year.

USS *Essex* and British Frigates in the Bay of Valparaiso
(print by unknown artist)

USS *Essex* at Nuka Hiva
(William Bainbridge Hoff)

Horn and put into Valparaiso, Chile, with two captured British whaling schooners. Over the next few months, the *Essex* captured thirteen more British whalers off the South American coast.

On March 3, Admiral George Cockburn arrived in Lynnhaven Bay, Virginia, with his squadron of British warships. His ships patrolled the offshore waters, fiercely attacking American vessels and frequently raiding U.S. coastal ports.

On March 19, Sir James Yeo was sent to Canada to command the British naval forces in the Great Lakes. He arrived in Quebec in May and immediately set about building vessels specifically suited for action on the lakes. To counter this threat, Lieutenant (later Commodore) Oliver Hazard Perry was appointed chief naval officer in charge of building an

Sir George Cockburn, Major General of Marines (print by unknown artist)

Oliver Perry, September 10, 1813 (engraving by Isaac Sanford)

Oliver Hazard Perry (oil by Edward L. Mooney)

American fleet on Presque Isle Bay at Erie, Pennsylvania. His subsequent battle actions would earn him the title "Hero of Lake Erie."

By the end of March, the British naval blockade extended from Long Island to Mississippi. Raiding parties went ashore often to capture supplies and disrupt trade. They were particularly aggressive in and around the Chesapeake Bay.

On April 6, the British bombarded the trading port of Lewes, Delaware, but did little damage. A cannonball is still lodged in the foundation of Cannonball House, now the city's maritime museum.

On April 13, American general James Wilkinson, former governor of the Louisiana Territory, captured Mobile in what was then Spanish West Florida, allowing American troops to occupy most of the coastal areas of today's Louisiana, Mississippi, Alabama, and Florida. Many years later, it was discovered that Wilkinson had been a secret agent for the Spanish, known as Agent 13.

On April 27, an American force backed by several ships landed on the northern shore of Lake Ontario and attacked York (now Ontario). The troops quickly routed the British from the fort to the west of the town and then seized the town and dockyard. As the British retreated, they blew up a warship under construction and the fort's magazine. The explosion killed thirty-eight Americans, including the commander,

Brigadier General Zebulon Pike, and wounded more than two hundred others. For the next three days, the Americans plundered York and burned many government buildings and homes. It was later claimed that the British burned Washington because of the Americans' actions in York.

While the Battle of York was only a minor American victory, it was important because artillery pieces and other ordnance captured there later played a decisive role against the British at the Battle of Lake Erie.

On May 1, British troops supported by Native American warriors and artillery attacked Fort Meigs in northwestern Ohio. The action was an attempt to delay any attack by the Americans to recapture Detroit. When the initial attack failed, the British laid siege to the fort. On May 5, the Americans sent out a large raiding party under Colonel William Dudley to spike the British guns. This objective achieved, many Americans charged into the woods, only to be cut down by Native American fire. The American troops that had remained by the British guns were quickly overrun by a counterattack and surrendered. Of the 866 officers and men who took part in the raid, only 160 survived. The incident became known as Dudley's Massacre. Some of the Americans who were taken prisoner were killed by Indians with apparently no attempt by the British to stop them. On May 7, terms were agreed upon for the exchange of all prisoners and the siege was abandoned.

On May 3, Admiral Cockburn attacked Havre de Grace, Maryland, at the mouth of the Susquehanna River. The action was notable because of Lieutenant John O'Neill, who single-handedly manned a cannon to try to stop the advance. He was wounded and captured by the British but quickly released. In gratitude, O'Neill and his descendants were made hereditary keepers of the Concord Point Lighthouse.

On May 27, the Americans defeated the British at the Battle of Fort George in Upper Canada. The fort, situated on the bank of the Niagara River near its mouth, was the westernmost British fort on Lake Ontario. After the capture of York, the American forces regrouped at Fort Niagara with the aim of attacking Fort George next. Lieutenant Perry helped reconnoiter landing sites and mark safe channels with buoys.

The American force consisted of about four thousand men supported by fourteen ships, all armed with cannon. On May 25, the ships started to bombard Fort George. Just after dawn on May 27, under the cover of fog, the Americans started to land. The British commander, Brigadier

View of Fort Niagara on Lake Ontario from the Lighthouse on the British Side
(engraving by Hewitt)

General John Vincent, had split up his troops to try to protect his entire front, but he committed most of them along the Niagara River, believing that was where the enemy would come ashore. The Americans, however, landed on the shores of the lake and were able to break through the defensive lines. Vincent ordered the fort's guns to be spiked and then retreated with his men to Queenston. The British tasked with carrying out his orders were presumably also anxious to escape and botched their task, so the Americans were able to take the fort almost intact.

Following the loss of Fort George, Vincent pulled back all his troops along the Niagara River, including Fort Erie, which was also abandoned on May 27 and occupied by the Americans. The troops were ordered to withdraw to Burlington Heights, a British army post in what is now Hamilton, Ontario.

On May 29, the British attacked Sackets Harbor, New York, which had become the U.S. Navy's Great Lakes headquarters and was a major shipbuilding center employing more than three thousand men. Because of its strategic importance on Lake Ontario and an attack the previous year that had been repulsed, the town was heavily fortified. The British troops were led by Sir George Prevost, commander in chief of British forces in North America, with Commodore Yeo in charge of the naval units. The attack was badly planned, and because of fierce resistance, neither British commander was prepared to totally commit his forces and so withdrew.

On June 1, HMS *Shannon*, commanded by Admiral Sir Philip Bowes Vere Broke, engaged the USS *Chesapeake* off Boston. Both were thirty-eight-gun frigates, and they were evenly matched.

Sir Philip Bowes Vere Broke
(print of an engraving by
J. Blood)

The *Shannon* had been patrolling offshore while the *Chesapeake* had been undergoing a refit in Boston Harbor. While the *Chesapeake* readied for sea, Broke of the *Shannon* sent a messenger ashore with a challenge to come out and fight:

> As the *Chesapeake* appears now ready for sea, I request you will do me the favor to meet the *Shannon* with her, ship to ship, to try the fortune of our respective flags. The *Shannon* mounts twenty-four guns upon her broadside and one light boat-gun; 18 pounders upon her main deck and 32-pounder carronades upon her quarter-deck and forecastle; and is manned with a complement of 300 men and boys, beside thirty seamen, boys, and passengers, who were taken out of recaptured vessels lately. I entreat you, sir, not to imagine that I am urged by mere personal vanity to the wish of meeting the *Chesapeake*, or that I depend only upon your personal ambition for your acceding to this invitation. We have both noble motives. You will feel it as a compliment if I say that the result of our meeting may be the most grateful service I can render to my country; and I doubt not that you, equally confident of success, will feel convinced that it is only by repeated triumphs in even combats that your little navy can now hope to console your country for the loss of that trade it can no longer protect. Favor me with a speedy reply. We are short of provisions and water, and cannot stay long here.[26]

---

26. Joseph Allen, *Battles of the British Navy*, Vol. 2 (London: Henry G. Bohn, 1852), 425.

James Lawrence
(print by Gilbert Stuart,
engraving by
David Edwin)

HMS *Shannon* Awaiting the Approach of USS *Chesapeake*
(print of an engraving by Robert Dodd)

Captain James Lawrence of the *Chesapeake* probably never got the
message, but he was anxious to break out of the harbor and put to sea.

The two ships met at half past five in the afternoon and opened fire
just before 6 p.m. about 115 feet apart. Broke had trained his gunners to be
excellent shots, and the *Chesapeake* was soon crippled, with many of her

HMS *Shannon* Firing the First Broadside at USS *Chesapeake*
(J. C. Schetky, lithograph engraving by L. Haghe)

USS *Chesapeake* Crippled by HMS *Shannon*
(J. C. Schetky, lithograph engraving by L. Haghe)

USS *Chesapeake* Is Captured by HMS *Shannon*
(J. C. Schetky, lithograph engraving by L. Haghe)

Boarding of the *Chesapeake* by the Crew of the *Shannon*
(print of an engraving by unknown artist)

USS *Chesapeake* vs.
HMS *Shannon*
(J. C. Schetky,
lithograph engraving
by L. Haghe)

crew killed or injured. Led by Broke, the British boarded the *Chesapeake*, and a vicious battle took place before they controlled the ship. The battle had lasted just eleven minutes.

The *Shannon* lost twenty-three men and the *Chesapeake* sixty, including Lawrence. His famous last words were "Don't give up the ship." The British buried him with full military honors. The action was the bloodiest naval engagement of the war, and all the more alarming in that it all took place in so short a time. The *Chesapeake*, with a prize crew aboard, was taken to Halifax, repaired, and recommissioned into the Royal Navy.

After Vincent had withdrawn his troops to Burlington Heights, he sent Lieutenant Colonel John Harvey to scout the American positions. The Americans under General Henry Dearborn had not followed up on their advantage by pursuing Vincent, but had decided to camp at Stoney Creek; General John Chandler then took over command. Harvey reported back to Vincent that the American lines were spread wide with few sentries. He recommended a night attack.

On June 5, just before midnight, the British troops left Burlington Heights. They killed the American sentries on the camp's outer perimeter, but as they were advancing silently, a group of Vincent's staff officers who were observing, elated by the men's progress, let out a cheer that alerted the Americans who were holding the high ground. The Americans had also changed their ammunition and were firing what in effect were shotgun cartridges, which decimated the British charges. However, a single order changed the course of the battle. General

William Winder moved troops to protect his left flank, which created a hole in the defenses and left their artillery unprotected. The British quickly realized this and bayonet-charged, overrunning the gun positions. In the confusion, General Chandler rode into the middle of the British troops and was captured. Shortly afterward, the same fate befell General Winder. The Americans counterattacked and were beaten back and fired upon by their own side.

The engagement lasted less than forty-five minutes. Even in defeat, the Americans never realized that they vastly outnumbered the enemy. Apart from capturing ordnance and supplies, the British had managed to push the Americans back. They would never advance that far again into Upper Canada.

On June 8, as the Americans retreated from Stoney Creek, they were bombarded at Forty Mile Creek by a British flotilla commanded by Commodore Yeo and harried on the ground by Canadian militia and Native American warriors. The Americans abandoned their position and retreated to Fort George. The next day, the Americans abandoned Fort Erie.

On June 20, the USS *Constellation*, trapped in Chesapeake Bay, unsuccessfully attempted to capture Royal Navy warships that were blockading Hampton Roads, Virginia. Two days later, a British force of more than seven hundred Royal Marines and soldiers landed west of Craney Island with the aim of taking Norfolk and the Gosport Navy Yard. As the British tried to cross the water to the mainland they came under withering fire from a much smaller American contingent and retreated. The British then attacked by barge, but were driven back again by artillery fire. Admiral Cockburn, who was in charge of blockading the Chesapeake Bay, called off the attack and withdrew his men.

On June 24, former French prisoners of war recruited by the British viciously attacked Hampton, Virginia, and over two days burned the town down. A British officer noted in his diary, "Every horror was perpetrated with impunity—rape, murder, pillage—and not a single man was punished."

The Battle of Beaver Dams also took place on June 24. An American column had been sent out from Fort George to make a surprise attack on Beaver Dams, a British outpost at Thorold, Ontario. They camped overnight at Queenston, and when they resumed their march the next morning they were attacked by about three hundred Mohawk Indians.

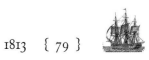

The Americans surrendered when a small detachment of British soldiers arrived on the scene having been alerted by Laura Secord, a resident of Queenston. Almost five hundred Americans were taken prisoner in what was a decisive British victory. A major result of the battle was that senior officers at Fort George stopped sending out patrols more than a mile from the fort.

On June 27, the American privateer *Young Teazer* was cornered in Mahone Bay, Nova Scotia. Rather than surrender the ship, Frederick Johnson, the first lieutenant, blew her up, killing almost the entire crew. The *Young Teazer* was one of the most successful privateers in the War of 1812 and was named after the *Teazer*, which had been captured by the British in December 1812 and set on fire. On her first voyage, the *Teazer* had captured twelve foreign ships, which were sent to U.S. ports as prizes.

On July 3, the sloops USS *Growler* and *Eagle* were captured by the British while on patrol near Île-aux-Noix on Lake Champlain. The *Growler* was renamed the *Shannon* by the Royal Navy and recaptured by the Americans at the Battle of Lake Champlain in September 1814.

On July 5, Fort Schlosser and its American garrison were attacked by the British. The fort, originally built by the British, was strategically important as it guarded the portage around Niagara Falls.

On July 8, Fort Madison was besieged by Sauk and other tribes allied with the British. After several weeks, the Americans finally abandoned the fort at night, burning it down and escaping by boat.

Also on July 8, a small detachment of British troops and Native Americans was sent to Butler's Farm at Two Mile Creek to recover a large consignment of medical supplies that had been buried when the British forces retreated after the Battle of Fort George. As they were loading the supplies, they were attacked by an American force. More American troops arrived and the British withdrew, pursued by Lieutenant Samuel Eldridge and about forty soldiers. They didn't realize they were being led into an ambush. Within minutes, twenty-three men had been killed—including Eldridge—or injured.

On July 26, the siege of Fort Meigs was finally lifted. The first siege had started on May 1 and lasted until May 9. Fort commander General Harrison then rode out, leaving General Green Clay in charge. The British then returned and laid siege to the fort again until July 26. After they withdrew, Harrison ordered that the fort be destroyed.

The Battle of Burnt Corn was fought on July 27 in Escambia County,

Alabama. Peter McQueen, a Creek Indian, allied his tribe to the British and in return was given money to buy supplies and ammunition from the Spanish governor of West Florida. When the Americans heard about this, they sent out a force from Fort Mims, north of Mobile. The Indians were ambushed as they made camp on the banks of Burnt Corn Creek. They fled into the surrounding swamps, and the American troops, dropping their guard, started to loot the supplies. The Indians then regrouped and counterattacked, forcing the Americans to retreat.

On July 31, the British raided the Champlain Valley and burned many buildings in Plattsburgh, on the shores of Lake Champlain.

On August 2, General Procter attacked Fort Stephenson in what is now Fremont, Ohio, using gunboats to soften the American defenses. Thinking the walls had been breached, he ordered his men to attack. The men descended into a wide trench surrounding the fort without realizing that the Americans had the trench covered by cannons. More than 150 British soldiers were killed, and the rest retreated. Procter abandoned the attack the following morning.

On August 4, Commodore Perry's Great Lakes fleet sailed into Lake Erie ready to do battle with the British.

On August 5, the American privateer *Decatur*, under Captain Dominique Diron, was on patrol off Bermuda when she spotted the HMS *Dominica*, a schooner captained by young Lieutenant George Barrete, escorting a merchant ship, the *Princess Charlotte*. None of the vessels were flying colors, so for over an hour they sailed side by side as Diron tried to identify the nationality of the other ships. Just after noon, Barrete raised the British flag and tried to outrun the *Decatur*. Realizing this was not possible, Barrete opened fire and a vicious battle ensued. The two ships were firing so close to each other that each captain could hear the other shouting orders. Despite having fewer guns, the American gunners gradually gained the upper hand, as they were more accurate. The *Dominica* tried to sail away, but was chased down by the *Decatur* and boarded. Barrete, despite being mortally wounded, never surrendered and continued to fight with his sword until he dropped dead. Although both ships were badly damaged, the *Dominica* was escorted into Charleston. The *Princess Charlotte* escaped.

On August 7, the U.S. Navy schooners *Hamilton* and *Scourge* ran into a storm off Fourteen Mile Creek, near Hamilton, Ontario, and sank with the loss of more than eighty lives. Both ships were merchant

Gun Crew of the *Scourge*
(acrylic on canvas by Erick Marshall Murray)

schooners that had been converted to warships, and the extra weight of the cannons and other reinforcements is thought to have affected their seaworthiness. The location of the sunken ships is a national historic site of Canada.

On August 10, after several days of the American and British naval forces in the Great Lakes playing cat and mouse, the British fleet stopped off Twelve Mile Creek. The American fleet consisted of two squadrons: one led by the USS *Julia* that included the USS *Pert*, and the other led by the USS *Pike*. As the American ships closed, the wind changed, giving the British the maneuvering advantage. Four American schooners were captured.

On August 14, the USS *Argus* was captured off the English coast. A few weeks earlier, William Crawford, the U.S. minister to France, had disembarked at L'Orient, and the ship had then taken up its station patrolling the English Channel. When she was spotted, she was no match for the British guns and was out of action within fifteen minutes. Her master, Captain William Allen, had his right leg blown off by a cannonball, but he stayed at his post until he collapsed from loss of blood and then died.

The Fort Mims Massacre took place on August 30 and was a reprisal for the Americans' attack on Peter McQueen and his "Red Stick" Creek

Indians at the Battle of Burnt Corn. The day before, two slaves had reported spotting "painted warriors" in the area, but scouts could find no trace of them; one of the slaves was flogged for raising a false alarm. Major Daniel Beasley, the fort commander, did not take any extra precautions, and at the time of the attack—during the midday meal— one of the main gates was partially open. Beasley was mortally wounded by a tomahawk as he tried to close the gate. The American troops and settlers who had sought refuge in the fort took up defensive positions in the inner enclosure, but the Indians set fire to the buildings and stormed inside. The death toll was close to five hundred with more than 250 scalps taken. The African American slaves were taken as slaves by the Creek.

THE BATTLE OF LAKE ERIE

September 10 saw the pivotal Battle of Lake Erie. Oliver Hazard Perry's brilliant victory raised the morale of the nation and put the Northwest Territory firmly under American control.

The background of the battle began in September 1812, when Secretary of the Navy Paul Hamilton authorized the building of four gunboats at Presque Isle, Pennsylvania, on Lake Erie. Captain Isaac Chauncey was sent from New York City to Sackets Harbor near the Thousand Islands at the east end of Lake Ontario. His orders were to take control of the Great Lakes. As commander of naval forces on the Upper Lakes, he worked with Sailing Master Daniel Dobbins to build a fleet of ships to accomplish this. Chauncey's second in command, Master Commandant Jesse Elliott, was in charge of naval forces in Lake Erie, and he began converting five small merchant ships into gunboats at Black Rock.

On New Year's Eve 1812, Chauncey visited Erie to inspect Dobbins's work. He ordered that two of the ships be lengthened and that two new brigs armed with carronades be built, the *Lawrence* and the *Niagara*. Most important, he requested that Hamilton appoint Perry as commander of the Erie squadron.

Building the fleet was a daunting task—all supplies had to be hauled overland from Pittsburgh or farther. Each frame was from a single tree, extending keel to main deck, which gave the vessels great strength. Local farmers were paid a dollar for each suitable tree. Because of a shortage of nails, much of their hulls was held together by wooden pins. Lead was used to caulk the hulls' seams.

Start of the Battle of Lake Erie
(Sully & Kearny, engraving by Murray Draper)

Battle of Lake Erie
(Sully & Kearny, engraving by Murray Draper)

Perry's Victory on Lake Erie
(engraving by John Warner Barber)

Southeast View of Sackett's Harbour
(print by Thomas Birch, engraving by W. Strickland)

The gun brigs *Niagara* and *Lawrence* were constructed at Cascade Shipyard. They were sister ships and built exactly alike:

- Length: 118 feet
- Beam: 30 feet
- Draft loaded: 9 feet
- Keel: black oak timber, 14 inches by 18 inches
- Planking: 3 inches thick of oak

- Length of gun deck: 100 feet
- Armament: 18 32-pounder carronades, plus 2 long 12-pounder guns
  (chasers well forward in bow)
- Square rigged two-masts and top-gallants
- Bulwarks: white pine
- Stanchions: red cedar and black walnut
- Gun ports: 36 inches square (10-foot centers)

Oliver Hazard Perry was born August 23, 1785, at Westerly, Rhode Island, of Quaker ancestors who left England in 1600. His father was a captain in the navy during the Revolution, and many of his male relatives reached senior positions in the U.S. Navy. Perry was an accomplished seaman by his early teens. On February 22, 1813, at the age of twenty-seven, he was promoted to commodore and set off for Erie.

He shared Dobbins's concerns about the lack of defenses and agreed with General David Mead to increase the number of troops and militia on Garrison Hill. Blockhouses were built around the shipyard to protect the unfinished vessels. The biggest threat, however, came from Canadian spies, who constantly passed on intelligence to the British military commanders. Little happened in Erie that they did not know about.

Perry's next concern was to get the fleet built. He made several trips to Pittsburgh to get supplies and recruit skilled carpenters, block makers, sail makers, and shipbuilders. It took fourteen wagons and fifty-six men over a month to haul thirty-seven carronades from Washington, D.C., where they were made at the foundry of George Foxall in Georgetown. Foxall pledged that if Perry won, he would build a church. Foundry United Methodist Church on 16th Street in Washington stands as proof of Perry's victory. A further twenty-eight carronades were sent from Sackets Harbor. The courthouse, the largest building in Erie, became the sail loft where the sails were cut and sewn together.

By April 1813, Perry's "Fleet in the Wilderness" was taking shape. *Tigress* and *Porcupine* were launched, followed in early May by *Scorpion*. The brig *Lawrence* was launched June 25 at the Cascade Yard, followed by *Niagara* and the pilot boat *Ariel* on July 4. The fleet was then joined by five converted merchant ships—*Somers*, *Trippe*, *Ohio*, *Caledonia*, and *Amelia*—which had sailed from Black Rock to Erie without being spotted by the British naval patrols; the *Amelia*, however, was considered unseaworthy and taken out of service. It had thus taken less than nine months to build and launch a fleet in the middle of a wilderness.

Most of the ships were crewed by farmers and settlers, so Perry spent August giving the men their sea legs. All the ships were seriously undermanned. On August 10, Elliott arrived with eighty-nine seamen. Perry promoted him to commodore and gave him command of the *Niagara*. When the fleet arrived at Put-in-Bay, Ohio, General Harrison had assembled a hundred expert Kentucky riflemen to serve as marines.

The British flotilla, based at Fort Malden, was commanded by Commodore Robert Barclay, an experienced and respected naval officer who had enlisted at the age of ten. He had been seriously wounded fighting alongside Admiral Lord Nelson at the Battle of Trafalgar and had lost an arm during another naval encounter with the French. When spies reported that the Americans were building the *Lawrence* and *Niagara*, Barclay ordered the construction of the *Detroit*, which became his flagship. Like Perry, Barclay had few experienced seamen, and requests for more men went unanswered. He had no marines, so he enlisted a motley group of soldiers, Canadian militia, and Native Americans. He knew that he could not take on the Americans until the *Detroit* was launched, yet his request for naval guns to arm her was ignored. He improvised by using nineteen guns from Fort Malden that had never been designed for use at sea.

While work on the *Detroit* continued, Perry used the time to train his crews. He also used his fleet to blockade Fort Malden so that supplies, normally brought in by ship, ran critically low. Barclay put to sea as quickly as he could for fear that if the blockade continued, the locals and Native Americans would turn against him. With the two fleets under way, a showdown was inevitable.

The Americans had more ships, but the British had more guns. The *Detroit*, with its long guns, had the overall advantage—they could be used long before any of the American ships were in range to fire.

Before leaving Erie, Perry had a blue flag with the words "Don't Give Up the Ship" made for hoisting at the start of action. These were the dying words of Perry's close friend, Captain James Lawrence, who three months earlier had been mortally wounded in the engagement between *Chesapeake* and *Shannon* near Boston.

At noon on September 10, both fleets were closing for action. Perry's fleet had the maneuvering advantage, and he planned on closing with the British quickly to take full advantage of the carronades' devastating raking fire and to avoid damage from the long guns. However, the *Detroit*

TABLE 4.1

AMERICAN SQUADRON			BRITISH SQUADRON		
9 vessels			6 vessels		
	Tons	*Guns*		*Tons*	*Guns*
Lawrence	260	20	*Detroit*	300	19
Niagara	260	20	*Queen Charlotte*	260	17
Caledonia	85	4	*Lady Prevost*	96	13
Ariel	60	3	*Brig Hunter*	75	10
Scorpion	60	2	*Little Belt*	60	3
Somers	65	2	*Chippewa*	35	1
Trippe	50	1	TOTAL	826	63
Porcupine	50	1			
Tigress	50	1			
TOTAL	940	54			

opened fire first when the fleets were about one and a half miles apart.

The American ships maintained formation and moved in to engage the enemy, except for the *Niagara*, commanded by Elliott, which failed to keep up.[27] The *Lawrence* was attacked by both the *Detroit* and *Queen Charlotte* and by 2:30 p.m. was unable to maneuver. Perry transferred to the *Niagara*, which had taken little part in the action. The British assumed that Perry was about to surrender, having lost his flagship, so they ceased firing.

Perry took command of the *Niagara* and sent Elliott in a small boat with orders to get the rest of the fleet back in formation. Perry then sailed straight through the British line, firing deadly broadsides at the *Lady Prevost* and *Chippewa* on his port side and the *Detroit* and *Queen Charlotte*, which had collided, on his starboard side. Within twenty minutes, the battle was over and the entire British fleet had surrendered. Perry sent his famous message to General Harrison: "We have met the enemy and they are ours—two ships, two brigs, one schooner and one sloop."

---

27. Why the *Niagara* stayed back at the beginning of the action remains a mystery. Perry suspected that Elliott resented him because Perry was put in charge of the fleet even though Elliott was the superior officer. Elliott claimed that they had not received any signals to attack. Their feud lasted the rest of their lives.

Naval War Heroes of the Battle of Lake Erie (lithograph by Nathaniel Currier)

Casualties on both sides were very heavy. Of the *Lawrence*'s crew of 103, 83 were killed or wounded. The British lost 135 killed or wounded.

Shortly after the battle, the twenty-eight-year-old Perry wrote to Secretary of the Navy William Jones:

U.S. Brig Niagara *off the West Sister Is., Head of Lake Erie,*
Sept. 10, 1813
4 P.M.

Sir:

It has pleased the Almighty to give to the arms of the United States a signal victory over their enemies on this Lake—the British squadron consisting of two ships, two brigs, one schooner and one sloop have this moment surrendered to the force under my command, after a sharp conflict.

I have the honor to be

Sir

Very respectfully

Your obedient servant

O.H. Perry

Perry's Victory (print by unknown artist)

The Battle of Lake Erie was a turning point in the war. Without naval power, the British lost control of the Great Lakes and western Canada. The British considered sending more troops to recapture the lost territory, but decided against it as they felt they needed to keep their resources at home in case there was further conflict in Europe.

Fall 1813

On September 25, the U.S. Navy scored another victory when the USS *Enterprise* captured HMS *Boxer* off Pemaquid Point, Maine. Captain Samuel Blythe of the *Boxer* was killed in the first fusillade, and Lieutenant William Burrows, captain of the *Enterprise*, was mortally wounded a few minutes later. The battle raged for thirty minutes as many of the British sailors deserted their posts. The *Enterprise* limped into Portland with its prize, which was little more than a wreck.

On September 26, Commodore Yeo left Burlington Bay on Lake Ontario with his British squadron of six vessels—two corvettes, a brig, and three schooners. An American fleet of eleven ships under Commodore Chauncey set sail the following day. On the morning of September 28, both

Naval Action on Lake Ontario, September 11, 1813
(drawing by Midshipman Peter Spicer)

Naval Action on Lake Ontario, August 10, 1813
(drawing by Midshipman Peter Spicer)

Action between USS *Enterprise* and HMS *Boxer*
(print by Carlton T. Chapman)

fleets lined up for battle off York. It was soon apparent that the British ships were outgunned, and Yeo made a dash for Burlington Bay, which was protected by British batteries on the surrounding cliffs. Chauncey gave chase, but called it off when he realized where the British ships were heading. The entrance to Burlington Bay was blocked by a sandbar, and it was partly though luck and partly through skilled seamanship that Yeo was able to navigate his ships into the bay. He was lucky because an exceptionally high tide gave his vessels extra depth. Chauncey had called off the chase, later to become known as the Burlington Races, because he thought the British ships would founder on the sandbar.

On October 5, the Americans won another decisive victory at the Battle of the Thames. For months, General Harrison and his Army of the Northwest had been battling British troops and Canadian militia as well as a confederation of Native American tribes led by Shawnee chief Tecumseh. The British depended on Lake Erie to bring in supplies and food by ship, so as soon as Harrison got news of Perry's victory, he knew the British would be forced to pull back, their supply lines cut. Harrison ordered an immediate advance, sending a thousand troops on horseback along the shores of Lake Detroit and using Perry's hastily repaired ships to ferry another 2,500 soldiers to Amherstburg.

Brigadier Procter, the British commander, had already abandoned Fort Amherstburg because food supplies had almost run out and all the cannons had been commandeered to arm the ill-fated British ships. Procter wanted to return to the British garrison at Burlington Heights, but Tecumseh persuaded him to stop at Moraviantown on the Thames River. Tecumseh knew that if the British troops returned to Burlington Heights, his tribes and their lands would have no protection against the Americans. Procter, however, gave no orders to defend his position and split his forces into two isolated groups. Morale among the soldiers, who were on half rations, was low.

Meanwhile, Harrison continued his push. On September 26, he retook Detroit and left a brigade to defend it. He also left a brigade to protect Sandwich and then set out to find Procter. The British retreat was poorly executed, and many British troops were captured after falling behind the main columns. On the evening of October 4, Harrison caught up with the rear guard of British troops and warriors and quickly overran them. A boat containing most of the British army's ammunition and food supplies was abandoned after it went aground and was captured by the Americans.

Just after dawn on October 5, the two sides met in battle. Harrison had overwhelming superiority in numbers—about 3,500 infantry and cavalry to Procter's 1,300 soldiers and warriors, who were already tired, hungry, and dispirited. Procter had just one cannon, which failed to fire as the American cavalry charged and broke through the British lines. Procter is said to have fled the field, and his troops surrendered immediately. Tecumseh and his warriors retreated into the swamp and fought on. The Americans finally overran their positions, and at some point, Tecumseh was killed in the fighting, which quickly ended Indian resistance.

The Americans burned down the settlement of Moraviantown, even though the peaceful Christian Munsee Indians who lived there had played no part in the fighting. More than six hundred British prisoners were taken. Procter was later court-martialed and found guilty of negligence and improper conduct.

This battle was significant because it reestablished American control over the Northwest Territory, and the death of Tecumseh effectively ended attacks by the tribes. Harrison signed an armistice with many of the chiefs at Detroit, which allowed him to send troops from Detroit east to combat the British along the Niagara River.

Meanwhile, in Europe, the Battle of Leipzig was fought on October 16 between Napoleon's army and the combined armies of Russia, Prussia, Austria, and Sweden. Napoleon's defeat ended his plans to conquer Europe, and he was forced to retreat to France. The following year, the allies would invade France, and Napoleon would be exiled to Elba. Napoleon's defeat at Leipzig raised hopes that the Napoleonic Wars could soon be over and that the British would seek to end the war with America. Less than a month later, the British in fact sought to start peace talks with the United States. They had several reasons for seeking peace. They wanted to pull back troops from North America to finish off Napoleon, and if they could negotiate a peace, America would be able to ship much-needed supplies to Britain and harass French merchant vessels.

In October, the Americans invaded Canada but were forced back at the Battle of Chateauguay. The aim was to capture Montreal. A force of four thousand men was dispatched in two columns. Unfortunately, the generals in charge of each column—Major General Wade Hampton and Major General James Wilkinson—had been feuding for years and were loath to help each other. Hampton's force from Burlington was supposed to march toward Odelltown, but he felt there were too many British in the area, so he marched west to Four Corners on the Chateauguay River, where he waited to hear news from Wilkinson's column, which had not yet set out. On October 18, he got news that Wilkinson was about to leave, so he advanced downriver.

While Hampton waited at Four Corners, the British had been able to gather their troops and send for reinforcements. The British and Canadians chopped down trees across the trails to slow the American advance while they dug in along the river. On October 25, Hampton decided to send out a brigade of about one thousand men, under the command of Colonel Robert Purdy, to cross the river at a ford. The aim was for these men to circle around behind the British positions while his main force attacked from the front. The Americans did not know that the ford was heavily defended, and as they started to cross on the morning of October 26, they came under heavy fire and were forced to retreat.

Coincidentally, after Purdy had set out, Hampton received orders that Wilkinson was now in charge of all American forces. With supplies running low, Hampton returned to Four Corners and waited for orders from Wilkinson.

Wilkinson and his men set out in bad weather for Grenadier Island at the head of the St. Lawrence, losing several boats along the way. Wilkinson did not receive the news about Hampton's defeat until November 6, and in the meantime he sent orders for Hampton to advance to Cornwall with enough supplies for both his own men and Wilkinson's column. As there were no supplies, Hampton decided to withdraw to Plattsburgh instead. He had already submitted his resignation, as he was not willing to serve under Wilkinson.

Unaware that Hampton was withdrawing, Wilkinson pressed on. He managed to land most of his troops on the south bank of the river and marched overland while his lightened boats sped past the British batteries at Fort Wellington in Prescott, Ontario, under the cover of darkness. The next morning, safely past the fort, the soldiers reembarked.

A British force had been dispatched from Kingston on November 7, and on November 9 its flotilla landed at Prescott. Wilkinson received news that the British column was advancing on him from the rear, so he landed his troops and set up his headquarters in Cook's Tavern. The British marched until they caught up with Wilkinson's rear guard on November 10. As it was late, they made camp at Crysler's Farm.

That same day, the Americans had driven off about five hundred Canadian militia during a skirmish at Hoople's Creek. Wilkinson decided that he needed to drive the British away before he continued his advance on Montreal.

At dawn on November 11, British gunboats started firing on the American positions and at 10:30 both sides lined up facing each other in battle formation. As Wilkinson was "indisposed," Brigadier General John Parker Boyd was commanding the American forces. Boyd finally ordered an attack in midafternoon, and the Americans were able to push the British back more than a mile. However, British troops had been positioned under cover for such an eventuality, and their volleys quickly forced the Americans to retreat. Another American flanking column ran into a British regiment; its two senior officers were killed almost immediately and the men retreated. As night fell and with the American army retreating in chaos, the British ceased their advance. Most of the

Americans were able to make it back to their boats and cross over to the southern banks of the river.

Wilkinson did press on toward Cornwall, where he received news that Hampton had been unable to get supplies and had returned to Plattsburgh. Wilkinson then called off the campaign and moved into winter quarters at French Mills, New York. American Brigadier General Leonard Covington, who had been mortally wounded during the Battle of Crysler's Farm, died at French Mills on November 14. Because of bad weather, shortage of supplies, and sickness among his men, Wilkinson was later forced back to Plattsburgh.

Meanwhile in the South, the Red Stick Creek were still attacking American settlements, so in October General Andrew Jackson led 2,500 Tennessee militia into the Mississippi Territory to root them out. On November 3, while some of his troops were constructing Fort Strother, a column was sent out to attack the nearby Creek village of Tallushatchee, where many Red Stick warriors were camped. More than 180 warriors were killed. Tennessee militiaman Davy Crockett, of Alamo fame, said later, "We shot them down like dogs."

On November 9, General Jackson's army attacked the Red Stick warriors who were besieging a friendly Creek village at Talladega. With heavy casualties on both sides, the Red Sticks were forced to retreat. With the onset of winter, the number of clashes reduced considerably.

A few days later, on November 13, at the Battle of Nanticoke, the militia of Norfolk, Ontario, put to flight a band of Native American warriors that had been attacking settlements and farms in that area.

Despite their naval losses in the Great Lakes and overtures of peace, the British ramped up the pressure on November 16 by implementing a naval blockade along the U.S. Atlantic coast.

During the early part of December, the British continued to withdraw most of their troops from Upper Canada. As they withdrew, the Americans moved in, reoccupying towns and destroying the farms of those people they suspected of supporting the British. Hearing about this, Major General John Vincent, the senior British officer in the field, ordered a small contingent back into the area to protect the loyalists. They set up base at Forty Mile Creek and then set out to chase the American troops down. The British cavalry charged the Americans near Twenty Mile Creek, scattering them, and most were taken prisoner. As the British neared Fort George, its commanding officer, Brigadier

General George McClure, decided to withdraw across the Niagara River to Fort Niagara.

On December 10, rather than let the nearby town of Newark, Ontario, fall into British hands, the Americans burned it to the ground. The inhabitants were ordered out of their homes, which were burned with all their possessions. The following morning, many families were found frozen to death in snowdrifts. The British reoccupied Fort George and vowed to get revenge for the destruction and death in Newark. The American officer in charge of the burning was court-martialed and dismissed from the army.

Fort Niagara across the river was now vulnerable. The commanding officer, Captain Nathaniel Leonard, was a habitual drunk and had done nothing to repair the fort's outer defenses damaged during bombardments in 1812 and early 1813. Most of the men under his command were ill or convalescing.

Lieutenant General Gordon Drummond, who was now lieutenant general for Upper Canada, ordered boats to be sent from Burlington. So as not to alert the Americans, they were dragged overland on sledges for the last leg of their journey to Fort George.

On the night of December 18, a force of about 550 British soldiers crossed the river and captured American outpost sentries, who were forced to tell them the American passwords. A small group of British approached the gate, gave the correct password, and were admitted. Within minutes, the rest of the British troops had rushed in. Two groups of American soldiers barricaded themselves in buildings and fought back. When they refused to surrender, the British showed them no mercy and most were bayoneted to death.

With Fort Niagara in their hands, the British, under the command of Major General Phineas Riall, accompanied by Native American warriors, set out to revenge the Newark attack. They burned almost every village and outpost along the southern side of the river, including Lewiston and Fort Schlosser, and killed and scalped many settlers. On December 30, Riall's men attacked and defeated American forces at the Battle of Buffalo, after which they burned the villages of Black Rock and Buffalo and destroyed the naval yard on Buffalo Creek.

FIVE

1814

As the war dragged on into a new year, General Andrew Jackson continued his campaign against the Red Stick Creek Indians. On January 22, he was camped close to Emuckfau Creek, north of Horseshoe Bend, Alabama, when he was attacked by a large force of Red Stick warriors. He beat off the attack, but discovered when he sent out scouts that the Red Stick village at Tohopeka at Horseshoe Bend—which was where he was heading—was too heavily fortified to attack. Jackson decided to return to Fort Strother, chased by Red Sticks.

On the evening of January 23, he camped at Enotachopco Creek. The Red Sticks attacked early the next day after they had left camp and were crossing the deep creek. Jackson had to rally his troops several times before they gained the upper hand in bloody hand-to-hand combat. While not winning an outright victory, Jackson inflicted heavy casualties on the Red Sticks and forced them to withdraw. Jackson then marched his men back to Fort Strother.

On March 27, his army rested and trained, Jackson moved on their main stronghold at Horseshoe Bend. He used his cannon for two hours to soften up the enemy and then ordered a bayonet charge. The battle was fought for five hours before Jackson secured a decisive victory. More than 550 Creeks were killed, many more drowned trying to cross the Tallapoosa River, and the remainder fled south into Spanish Florida. The Red Sticks would no longer be a problem.

Both the American and British armies curtailed most military activity during the harsh winter, but on March 4 the Battle of Longwoods took place near Wardsville, Ontario. The Americans had sent out a mounted raiding party under the command of Captain Andrew Holmes to capture one of the British outposts at Delaware or Port Talbot on Lake Erie. After a skirmish with Canadian militia from Port Talbot, Holmes headed for Delaware. On March 2, he was fifteen miles from Delaware when he learned that a strong British column from there was less than an hour away. He withdrew to Twenty Mile Creek and dug in on the high ground.

On March 4, the British advance guard attacked and tried to draw the Americans out into an ambush without success. Late in the afternoon, the full British force, including Canadian militia and Indians, attacked. The Americans, though heavily outnumbered, had chosen their defensive positions well, and the British were forced into a narrow corridor where they were cut down by American fire. Those who made it to the foot of the hill could not climb it because of the ice and the heavy fire aimed at them. At nightfall, the British retreated. Holmes, realizing that he was still outnumbered, called off the attack on Delaware and returned to Detroit.

Major General James Wilkinson had been wintering with his army at French Mills, just inside the U.S. border in New York, when he was ordered to send a division to reinforce Sackets Harbor and withdraw with the rest of his troops to Plattsburgh. They were followed by the British, who gathered up supplies that had been left in settlements such as Four Corners or abandoned along the way.

Wilkinson was determined to restore his reputation following his defeat at Crysler's Farm and decided to attack a British outpost at Lacolle Mills, a few miles to the north, which was defended by a small garrison of about eighty men. Wilkinson left Plattsburgh on March 27 with four thousand men and artillery, but thick snow slowed his progress, and they didn't arrive at Lacolle Mills until March 30. He attacked in the afternoon but the sound of the gunfire attracted other British and Canadian militia in the area who raced to the scene. At the same time, British gunboats were also firing on the American positions. The Americans were making little headway as night fell, so Wilkinson ordered a retreat back to Plattsburgh. A month later, he was relieved of his command, but a subsequent court-martial found him not guilty of negligence and misconduct.

In Europe, Britain and its allies had captured Paris. On April 11, Napoleon was forced to abdicate. He was exiled to the island of Elba, although he was to escape the following year, return to France, where the king had fled, and prepare to go on the offensive again. But now, with Napoleon defeated and in exile, the United States repealed the ineffective Embargo Act and Nonimportation Act on April 14 in the hope that it might stimulate peace talks. The British responded by sending an additional sixteen thousand troops to North America and on April 25 by blockading the New England ports.

The naval war was heating up. On March 28, the USS *Essex*, a thirty-six-gun frigate that had been trapped in the neutral Valparaiso, Chile, harbor by British warships for several weeks, decided to make a run for sea. As she sailed into open waters, she lost her main topmast in a storm and was quickly set upon by HMS *Phoebe* and *Cherub*. The Battle of Valparaiso raged for nearly three hours. After catching fire, the *Essex* surrendered. More than a third of her crew was killed and thirty-one went missing as they jumped overboard during the fire and tried to swim ashore. The *Essex* was repaired and recommissioned into the Royal Navy as HMS *Essex*.

The USS *Frolic*, which had left Boston on February 18 for a patrol in the West Indies, sank a British merchant ship and a Spanish privateer on March 28, and on April 3 sank another British merchant ship. While sailing in the Florida Strait on April 20, the *Frolic* was spotted by HMS *Orpheus*, a thirty-six-gun frigate, and the twelve-gun schooner HMS *Shelburne*, which gave chase. The *Frolic* managed to outrun the enemy for six hours, but was overhauled a few miles off the coast of Cuba and surrendered. She was then commissioned into the Royal Navy as HMS *Florida*.

On April 28, the USS *Peacock* was on patrol in the Atlantic off Florida. She had earlier broken through the blockade of New York harbor to deliver supplies to St. Marys, Georgia. She was then supposed to join up with the USS *President*, but the latter had been unable to break out of New York so the *Peacock* went on patrol looking for British merchant ships sailing north from the West Indies. In the evening, she saw on the horizon a number of ships escorted by HMS *Epervier*. As the merchant ships sailed away, the *Epervier* closed to do battle.

USS *Peacock* in Action against HMS *Epervier*
(oil by Tomiro)

Peacock and *Epervier*
(print by Thomas Birch, engraving by Abel Bowen)

The two warships engaged the following morning. The *Epervier* was outgunned and after forty minutes was badly damaged and taking on water. Her captain, Commander Richard Wales, tried to organize boarding parties to take the *Peacock*, but his crew refused and he was obliged to surrender. The *Peacock*'s boarding party was able to repair the damage quickly, and the *Epervier* was escorted into Savannah, Georgia, a few days later.[28]

On May 1, General William Clark (of Lewis and Clark fame), the governor of the Missouri Territory, left St. Louis for Prairie du Chien, a strategic settlement at the confluence of the Mississippi and Wisconsin rivers. The area had been granted to the United States in the Treaty of Paris in 1783, but little had been done to establish an American presence. As the War of 1812 dragged on, American military commanders realized that they needed troops in the area to prevent the British from attacking

---

28. It turned out that the battle was even more one sided than it appeared. Captain Wales had done almost no gun drills with his crew, and many of the cannons had not been fired before they went into action against the *Peacock*. When they were fired for the first time, most of the cannons fell off their gun carriages and were useless. Many of the crew were later court-martialed for failing in their duty to fight.

from Canada. General Clark marched up the Mississippi and ordered work to begin on Fort Shelby in Prairie du Chien.

Fort Oswego, close to Oswego, New York, was a small outpost but an important one, as it protected the American supply route through New York to Sackets Harbor. On May 3, Commodore Sir James Yeo's squadron of eight British frigates, sloops, and gunboats sailed from Kingston, arriving off Oswego on May 5. However, a sudden violent squall forced them to call off any action until the following day. The Americans, having seen the ships arrive, spent the night moving their guns so they all faced the lake.

On the morning of May 6, the British frigates HMS *Prince Regent* and *Princess Charlotte* started to bombard the fort, while the smaller guns on the other vessels in the squadron were used to clear the beaches and surrounding woods. When the British troops tried to land, they found themselves jumping into deep water, and their ammunition got wet and became useless. Nevertheless, they fixed bayonets and charged. The American defenders ran away, abandoning the fort and leaving behind many injured who were taken prisoner. The British not only took possession of large quantities of food but also captured a number of ships, including the USS *Growler*, which had been captured by the British a year before and then recaptured by the Americans. On board the *Growler* were several cannons. The British took what supplies they could and burned the fort, barracks, and remaining supplies.[29]

On May 14, the struggle for control of Lake Champlain began with the Battle of Otter Creek. A Royal Navy flotilla led by the brig HMS *Linnet* took up position behind Providence Island waiting for the American fleet to sail out of Otter Creek, Vermont. The Americans also had land guns protecting the mouth of the creek. When the British ships moved in, they were bombarded by cannon and rifle fire from the Vermont militia. The British lost many men killed and wounded and withdrew to Île-aux-Noix. A few days later, the American fleet left Otter Creek without incident and sailed to Cumberland Bay off Plattsburgh.

---

29. During the winter, the British and Americans had each begun building two warships to try to gain naval superiority. The British built the frigates *Prince Regent* and *Princess Charlotte* and first used them at the Battle of Fort Oswego. Commodore Chauncey's ships took longer because they were bigger, but once launched, they gave him control of Lake Ontario.

Naval Action on Lake Champlain
(print by Read)

On May 18, Lieutenant Colonel Robert McDouall, who had been aide-de-camp to Governor General Prevost and later rose to the rank of major general, took over as commanding officer of Fort Mackinac on Mackinac Island in Lake Huron. The fort, an important American trading post, had been captured early in the war, but after the Battle of Lake Erie, it had become isolated. McDouall brought with him vital supplies and started to reinforce the fort and the island.

On May 29, Commodore Yeo was patrolling off the southern shores of Lake Ontario looking for American troops and supply trains. At the same time, an America flotilla of nineteen bateaux carrying cannons and supplies was attempting to reach Sackets Harbor. At Sandy Creek, the Americans waited for troops to arrive to escort them into Sackets Harbor. A bateau that had fallen far behind was captured by the British, and the crew revealed where the rest of the flotilla was. A force of seven British gunboats was sent after the flotilla.

As the British sailed into Sandy Creek, they came under fire from American shore batteries, American riflemen, and Oneida warriors. The British tried to retreat, but their boats were trapped and they were forced to surrender. What was meant to be a minor skirmish resulted in a significant win for the Americans as Yeo lost seven boats and crews, and Commodore Chauncey acquired the guns he needed to arm his new warship, the USS *Superior*.

On June 6, with Fort Shelby under construction, General Clark returned to St. Louis, and Lieutenant Joseph Perkins was put in

Isaac Chauncey
(print by Joseph Wood,
engraving by
David Edwin)

command. On hearing this news on June 28, Colonel McDouall at Fort Mackinac ordered Lieutenant Colonel William McKay to put together an expedition to recapture Prairie du Chien and take the fort.

The same day, the USS *Wasp*, on patrol in the approaches to the English Channel, chased down HMS *Reindeer*. The battle lasted only nineteen minutes, according to the *Wasp's* log, but both ships made repeated attempts to board the other as opposing cannons raked the decks with deadly grapeshot. The *Wasp* won the day, and the *Reindeer* was set on fire and exploded. Her captain, Commodore William Manners, was among the twenty-five crewmen killed.

On July 3, the Americans retook Fort Erie, which they had abandoned in June 1813. They immediately set about strengthening its fortifications, which was a wise decision in view of subsequent events. The fort was recaptured by an American force of four thousand men commanded by General Jacob Brown, who had orders to cross the Niagara, march west, and seize York, the capital of Upper Canada.

Having retaken Fort Erie, Brown moved north to the Chippawa River, where the British had established their forward lines of defense. Concerned that the British might be moving up reinforcements, Brown attacked. His advancing troops ran straight into the main body of the British. The Americans had, however, posted riflemen at the end of open ground, and the British were cut down as they tried to cross. It was a costly battle for both sides, with hundreds dead and wounded. The British pulled back to Fort George, and Brown waited at Queenston for naval support that never arrived. Unwilling to press on without naval support, he pulled back to Chippawa.

In May, a series of trials—the Bloody Assize—started at Ancaster,

Upper Canada, with nineteen people accused of high treason for supporting the Americans. Fifteen were condemned to death, and on July 20, eight were hung at Burlington Heights. The remaining "traitors" were sentenced to exile.

Also on July 20, Fort Shelby surrendered to the British after a short siege. Colonel McKay's troops and many Native American warriors had arrived at the fort on July 17, and a note was sent to the fort calling for the Americans' immediate surrender. Lieutenant Perkins refused, and that afternoon the British started an artillery barrage. A wooden gunboat, the *Governor Clark*, was anchored in the Mississippi River close to the fort, but intense British fire forced it to retreat; otherwise, it would have been sunk. Unfortunately, the gunboat was carrying much-needed ammunition. By the third day, the Americans were low on ammunition and had run out of water. Perkins offered to surrender, but McKay asked him to wait one day so that he could send the warriors away to avoid a massacre. On July 20, the fort formally surrendered and was occupied by the British and renamed Fort McKay. Under the terms of surrender, the American troops were allowed to return to St. Louis.

One of the westernmost battles of the war was fought at Rock Island Rapids, on what is now Campbell's Island, Illinois, on July 21. Lieutenant John Campbell was in charge of a force of U.S. infantry protecting three gunboats on the Mississippi that were carrying supplies to Fort Shelby. One of the gunboats was also carrying wives and children of some of the soldiers. They were attacked by about five hundred pro-British Sauk warriors in their war canoes. Campbell was forced to turn back. This left the Sauk firmly in control of the area and five settlements that straddled the Mississippi—Davenport, Bettendorf, Rock Island, Moline, and East Moline—now known as the Quad Cities.

Also on July 21, the Americans raided Sault Ste. Marie, a small settlement and British trading post of the North West Company run by John Johnston, a British fur trader who had married the daughter of Chippewa chief Waub-o-jeeg. The Americans burned down the homes and storage sheds.

On July 22, the Treaty of Greenville was signed in Ohio between the United States and the Western Confederacy of tribes—the Wyandot, Delaware, Shawnee, Ottawa, Seneca, Potawatomi, Kickapoo, and Miami. The tribes pledged to make peace with each other and to ally with the Americans against the British.

Three days later, on July 25, the Battle of Lundy's Lane (also known as the Battle of Niagara Falls) took place. After the Battle of Chippawa, the British had withdrawn to Fort George on Lake Ontario near the mouth of the Niagara River. General Brown moved his men to Queenston, a few miles to the south, but they were under frequent attack from raiding parties, so he withdrew to the Chippawa River. As soon as he moved out, he was shadowed by a British force, which advanced to Lundy's Lane, about four miles north of Brown's position. A second British column was also dispatched from Fort Niagara.

Brown did not realize the British were at Lundy's Lane, and he marched his troops north straight into their positions. The British had positioned their artillery and rocket detachments on the high ground, and the advancing Americans suffered high casualties under their fire. Brown sent a detachment of troops to outflank the British, and they surprised the British and Canadian units and put them to flight. Brown's main force was then able to capture the British guns and drive back their infantry. When the British counterattacked, there was confusion and they started firing on their own men. Just before midnight, the British launched a third and final counterattack, but were again driven back after hand-to-hand fighting, having suffered many casualties.

Both sides chose to withdraw from the battlefield. Brown withdrew to Fort Erie, and General Gordon Drummond withdrew to Queenston to await reinforcements. It was one of the bloodiest battles of the war. The British had inflicted heavy casualties on the Americans, but they failed to follow up their advantage and allowed the Americans to regroup and strengthen the fortifications at Fort Erie.

On July 26, Commodore Arthur Sinclair's squadron of five brigs and gunboats arrived off Mackinac Island with a force of seven hundred American soldiers. The American ships bombarded the island for two days with little effect. Fort George, which McDouall had hurriedly built on a ridge, was out of range of the guns. Fog then descended on the area, and the ships were forced to withdraw for a week before returning to disembark the soldiers.

As the Americans moved in on August 4, McDouall led his main force out of Fort Mackinac to a defensive line he had prepared earlier that lay in the path of the advance. The Americans were cut down, and troops sent to outflank the British were ambushed by warriors. The Americans retreated back to their boats, and Mackinac remained in British hands until the end of the war.

On August 4, peace negotiations between Britain and the United States began in Ghent while the two sides continued to battle it out in North America and on the high seas.

On August 9, the chiefs of the Creek nation signed the Treaty of Fort Jackson, formally ending the Creek War. Under the terms of the treaty, the Creek ceded twenty-three million acres of land in Alabama and Georgia to the U.S. government. More important, with a peace treaty signed, General Jackson was able to take his troops south to help defend Louisiana.

On August 10, a British naval squadron attacked the coastal village of Stonington, Connecticut. More than fifty tons of cannonballs, rockets, and missiles were fired at the village. After two days, the British sailed away. It is still a mystery why the village was singled out for attack.

On August 12, the schooner USS *Somers* and the USS *Ohio* were captured on Lake Ontario. The British rowed up to the two ships, pretending to be provision boats. They were able to scramble aboard and overpower the skeleton crews and sail off with their prizes.

On August 13, three warships from Sinclair's squadron—the *Niagara*, *Tigress*, and *Scorpion*—arrived at the mouth of the Nottawasaga River, where they waited for HMS *Nancy*, a lightly armed schooner used as a supply ship. The Americans thought the *Nancy* had not yet reached the river, and it was only when they sent a boat ashore to collect firewood that they realized the schooner was already there. On August 14, the crew of the *Nancy* set her on fire to prevent her being captured. The crew and her captain, Lieutenant Miller Worsley, escaped in small boats and rowed 360 miles to Fort Michilimackinac.

On August 14, the British occupied Pensacola, part of Spanish West Florida, because they needed it to stage attacks in the west.

On August 15, the British launched an all-out attack on Fort Erie. The Americans had heavily fortified their positions, and the British were further disadvantaged when a huge explosion killed more than a thousand of their men. The British called off the attack, but laid siege to the fort.

The Burning of Washington, D.C.

On August 19, a British invasion army under the command of General Robert Ross landed at Benedict on the Patuxent River in southern Maryland. From here, the British began their march on the U.S. capital.

About the same time, a British naval squadron approached the Potomac River.

Most of the members of President James Madison's cabinet did not think the British would attack Washington, and so little had been done to defend it—until it was too late. On August 22, Secretary of the Navy William Jones wrote the following letter to Master Commandant John O. Creighton, ordering him to gather as much intelligence as he could about the British advance. It shows how little information they had.

Sir,

The reports from the vicinity of Cedar Point yesterday, state that six ships of the enemy either had passed, or were at that time passing the Kettle Bottoms and ascending the Potomac. What the nature of his force is, or whether accompanied with transports or troops is quite uncertain.

It is desirable to ascertain by the discriminating eye of a naval officer the real extent & nature of this force as well as its probable object; whether it be to ascend the river, to act in conjunction with the invading army, or to create a diversion of our force from that army. You will therefore apply to Commodore Tingey, who will furnish you with a fast gig & crew with which you will proceed down the river & carefully reconnoiter the enemy, watching his movements & penetrating if possible his designs, which you will report to me by a trusty express over land, or in any other safe & expeditious manner, when you have completed your observations & satisfied yourself as far as may be practicable you will return to this city & report the result to this Department. I am respectfully &c.

W. Jones[30]

That same day, Brigadier General William Winder, commanding officer of the Tenth Military District, which included Washington and Baltimore, and about two thousand men, many of them poorly trained militia, skirmished with a British advance guard at Long Old Fields to the south. He was forced to retreat and decided to take a stand at Bladensburg, which controlled the roads to Baltimore and Annapolis. The roads were also being used to rush reinforcements and supplies into the capital.

---

30. U.S. Naval History and Heritage Command, *The Defense and Burning of Washington in 1814*, "Naval Preparations for the Defense of Washington," http://www.history.navy.mil/library/online/burning_washington.htm.

Barney's Sailors Serving as Artillerymen during the Battle
(watercolor by unknown artist)

Brigadier General Tobias Stansbury and his troops from Baltimore took up a commanding position on Lowndes Hill, just east of Bladensburg, and then he inexplicably marched his men down again to new positions on low ground across the Bladensburg Bridge. As more American regiments and artillery arrived, there was little discussion between the commanding officers, and as a result troops were positioned on exposed ground, too far away to protect the artillery, or too far from the next defensive position so that there were huge gaps in the line, sometimes as much as a mile or more. When Stansbury had crossed the river, he had not destroyed the bridge behind him and then had positioned his troops too far away to defend it. On top of this, the troops were tired from their forced marches, many were badly trained and equipped, and it was the middle of summer with very hot, humid weather.

The British reached Bladensburg around noon on August 24 and on their second charge were able to cross the bridge. The American artillery was firing cannonballs because it didn't have grapeshot, which would have cut the enemy down. And if Stansbury had stayed on the higher ground, he would have seriously disrupted the advance and might even have forced them back.

Captain Joshua Barney
(G. William after a miniature by Isabey)

Captain Joshua Barney
(painting by Stanislav Rembski)

The British pressed on with their advance, forcing some of the American artillery to withdraw. A gun battery from the naval dockyard, led by Captain (later Commodore) Joshua Barney, did hold up the advance for a time and cause major British casualties, but once they were captured, Winder ordered a retreat. The order did not get through to several units, though, who were quickly overrun and captured. Large numbers of militia deserted.

The Battle of Bladensburg was a shambles for the Americans and the rush to get away from the battlefield became known as the Bladensburg Races. The battle is regarded as the "greatest disgrace ever dealt to American arms."[31]

As President Madison and his cabinet fled the city along with most of its citizens, the British entered as night fell, raised the Union Jack, and set fire to most of the government buildings, including the White House and the Capitol. The Americans themselves set fire to the naval yard to prevent it, its stores, and the forty-four-gun frigate USS *Columbia* under construction from falling into enemy hands.

31. Daniel Walker Howe, *What Hath God Wrought: The Transformation of America* (New York: Oxford University Press, 2007).

On August 25, with fires still raging through the city, General Ross sent two hundred men to destroy 150 barrels of gunpowder that they had left behind in an abandoned fort on Greenleaf's Point. Many of the men were killed or seriously injured when the powder ignited.

Many of the fires were put out less than twenty-four hours later when a tornado and heavy rains hit Washington, killing both Americans and British and damaging many of the British troopships.

The burning of Washington was largely in retaliation for the Americans' burning and looting of York. It was also apparently meant purely for psychological impact on the Americans, because the British, having made their point, withdrew. The occupation of Washington lasted just over one day, and Madison and his government then returned.

On August 27, the British occupied Point Lookout, Maryland, where the Potomac River and Chesapeake Bay meet. On the same day, the American garrison at Fort Washington, overlooking the Potomac River, destroyed it before retreating.

Barney, who was badly wounded during the battle, later wrote the following letter to Navy Secretary Jones. It describes not only the battle but also the military code that operated at the time.

Farm at Elk Ridge. August 29th, 1814

Sir,

This is the first moment I have had it in my power to make a report of the proceedings of the forces under my command since I had the honor of seeing you on Tuesday the 23d. at the Camp at the "Old fields," on the afternoon of that day we were informed that the Enemy was advancing upon us. The Army was put into order of battle and our positions taken, my forces were on the right, flanked by the two Battalions of the 36 & 38th Regiments where we remained some hours. The enemy did not however make his appearance. A little before sun set, General Winder came to me and recommended that the heavy Artillery should be withdrawn with the exception of one 12 lb. to cover the retreat; We took up our line of march and in the night entered Washington by the Eastern branch Bridge, I marched my Men &c to the Marine Barracks and took up Quarters for the night, myself sleeping at Comr. Tingeys at the Navy yard, About 2 o' clock. General Winder came to my Quarters and we made some arrangements.

In the morning I received a note from General Winder and waited upon him, he requested me to take command, and place my Artillery to defend the passage of the Bridge on the Eastern Branch as the enemy was approaching the City in that direction, I immediately put my guns in Position, leaving the Marines & the rest of my men at the Barracks to wait further orders. I was in this situation when I had the honor to meet you, with the President, & heads of Departments, when it was determined I should draw off my Guns & men and proceed towards Bladensburg, which was Immediately put into execution; on our way I was informed the enemy was within a mile of Bladensburg we hurried on. The day was hot, and my men very much crippled from the severe marches we had experienced the preceding days before, many of them being without shoes, which I had replaced that morning. I preceded the men and when I arrived at the line which separates the District from Maryland the Battle began. I sent an officer back to hurry on my men, they came up in a trot, we took our position on the rising ground, put the pieces in Battery, posted the Marines under Capt. Miller and the flotilla men who were to act as Infantry under their own officers, on my right to support the pieces, and waited the approach of the Enemy. During this period the engagement continued, the enemy advancing, our own Army retreating before them apparently in much disorder. At length the enemy made his appearance on the main road, in force, and in front of my Battery, and on seeing us made a halt, I reserved our fire. In a few minutes the enemy again advanced, when I ordered an 18 lb. to be fired, which completely cleared the road, shortly after a second and a third attempt was made by the enemy to come forward but all were destroyed, The enemy then crossed over into an Open field and attempted to flank our right, he was there met by three twelve pounders, the Marines under Capt. Miller and my men acting as Infantry, and again was totally cut up. By this time not a vestige of the American Army remained except a body of 5 or 600 posted on a height on my right from whom I expected much support, from their fine situation. The Enemy from this period never appeared in force in front of us. They pushed forward their sharp shooters, one of which shot my horse under me, who fell dead between two of my Guns; the enemy who had been kept in check by our fire for nearly half an hour now began to outflank us on the right. Our guns were turned that way. He pushed up the Hill, about 2 or 300, towards the Corps of Americans stationed as above described, who, to my great mortification made no resistance, giving a fire or two and retired. In this situation we had the whole army of the Enemy

to contend with. Our Ammunition was expended and unfortunately the drivers of my ammunition wagons had gone off in the general panic. At this time I received a severe wound in my thigh, Capt. Miller, was wounded, Sailing Master Warner Killed, Acting sailing Master Martin killed, & Sailing Master Martin wounded, but to the honor of my officers & men, as fast as their Companions & mess mates fell at the guns they were instantly replaced from the Infantry. Finding the enemy now completely in our rear, and no means of defense, I gave orders to my officers and men to retire. Three of my officers assisted me to get off a short distance but the great loss of blood occasioned such a weakness that I was compelled to lie down. I requested my officers to leave me, which they obstinately refused, but upon being ordered they obeyed. One only remained. In a short time I observed a British soldier and had him called and directed him to seek an officer. In a few minutes an officer came. On learning who I was, he brought General Ross & Admiral Cockburn to me. Those officers behaved to me with the most marked attention, respect, and politeness, had a Surgeon brought and my wound dressed immediately. After a few minutes conversation the General informed me, (after paying me a handsome compliment) that I was paroled and at liberty to proceed to Washington or Bladensburg, as also was Mr. Huffington who had remained with me, offering me every assistance in his power, giving orders for a litter to be brought in which I was carried to Bladensburg. Capt Wainwright first Captain to Admiral Cochrane remained with me and behaved to me as if I was a brother.

During the stay of the enemy at Bladensburg I received the most polite attention from the officers of the Navy & Army.

My wound is deep, but I flatter myself not dangerous, the Ball is not yet extracted, I fondly hope a few weeks will restore me to health, and that an exchange will take place, that I may resume my Command or any other, that you and the President may think proper to honor me with, yours respectfully

Joshua Barney[32]

The British account was given in a letter sent by Rear Admiral George Cockburn to Vice Admiral Sir Alexander Cochrane.

32. U.S. Naval History and Heritage Command, *The Defense and Burning of Washington in 1814*, "Battle of Bladensburg and the Attack on Washington, 24–25 August 1814," http://www.history.navy.mil/library/online/burning_washington.htm.

Admiral Cochrane
(engraving by Ridley)

His Majesty's Sloop Manly *off Nottingham Patuxent*
27 August 1814

Sir

I have the honor to inform you that agreeably to the Intentions I notified to you in my Letter of the 22nd. Instant, I proceeded by Land on the Morning of the 23rd. to Upper Marlborough, to meet and confer with Major General Ross as to our further operations against the Enemy, and we were not long in agreeing on the propriety of making an immediate attempt on the City of Washington.

In Conformity therefore with the wishes of the General, I instantly sent orders for our Marine and Naval Forces at Pig Point, to be forthwith moved over to Mount Calvert, and for the Marines, Marine Artillery, and

a Proportion of the Seamen to be there landed and with the utmost possible expedition to join the Army, which I also most readily agreed to accompany.

The Major General then made his Dispositions, and arranged that Captain Robyns with the Marines of the Ships should retain possession of Upper Marlborough, and that the Marine Artillery and Seamen should follow the Army to the Ground it was to occupy for the Night. The Army then moved on, and bivouacked before dark about five Miles nearer Washington.

In the night Captain Palmer of the Hebrus, *and Captain Money of the* Trave, *joined us with the Seamen, and with the Marine artillery under Captain Harrison. Captain Wainwright of the* Tonnant *had accompanied me the day before, as had also Lieutenant James Scott (acting 1st. Lieutenant) of the* Albion.

At Daylight the morning of the 24th. the Major General again put the Army in Motion directing his March upon Bladensburg, on reaching which place, with the advanced Brigade, the Enemy was discovered drawn up in Force on a rising Ground beyond the Town, and by the Fire he soon opened on us as we entered the Place, gave us to understand he was well protected with Artillery; General Ross however did not hesitate in immediately advancing to attack him, although our Troops were almost exhausted with the Fatigue of the March they had just made, and but a small proportion of our little Army had yet got up; this dashing Measure was however, I am happy to add, crowned with the Success it merited, for in Spite of the galling Fire of the Enemy our Troops advanced steadily on both his Flanks and in his Front, and as soon as they arrived on even ground with him he fled in every direction, leaving behind him Ten Pieces of Cannon and a considerable Number of killed and wounded, amongst the latter Commodore Barney and Several other Officers. Some other Prisoners were also taken, though not many, owing to the Swiftness with which the Enemy went off, and the Fatigues our Army had previously undergone.

It would Sir be deemed presumption in me to attempt to give you particular details respecting the nature of this Battle, I shall therefore only remark generally that the Enemy, Eight thousand Strong, on Ground he had chosen as best adapted for him to defend, where he had had time to erect his Batteries and concert all his measures, was dislodged as Soon as reached, and a Victory gained over him by a Division of the British Army not amounting to more than Fifteen hundred Men headed by our Gallant

General whose brilliant achievement of this day it is beyond my Power to do justice to, and indeed no possible Comment could enhance.

The Seamen with the Guns were to their great mortification with the Rear Division during this Short but decisive action, those however attached to the Rocket Brigade were in the Battle, and I remarked with much pleasure the precision with which the Rockets were thrown by them under the Direction of 1st. Lieutenant Lawrence of the Marine artillery—Mr. Jeremiah. McDaniel Masters Mate of Tonnant *a very fine young man who has passed and who was attached to this party being Severely wounded, I beg permission to recommend him to your favorable Consideration. The Company of Marines I have on so many occasions had cause to mention to you, Commanded by 1st. Lieutenant Stephens, was also in the action, as were the Colonial Marines under the Temporary Command of Captain Reed of the 6th. West India Regiment, (these Companies being attached to the Light Brigade), and they respectively behaved with their accustomed Zeal and Bravery. None other of the Naval Department were fortunate enough to arrive up in Time to take their share in this Battle, excepting Captain Palmer of the* Hebrus, *with his Aid-de-Camp Mr. Arthur Wakefield Midshipman of that Ship, and Lieutenant James Scott 1st. of the* Albion, *who acted as my aid-de-Camp and remained with me during the whole Time.*

The Contest being Completely ended and the Enemy having retired from the Field, the General gave the Army about two hours rest, when he again moved forward on Washington; It was however dark before we reached that City, and on the General, myself and some officers advancing a short way past the first Houses of the Town without being accompanied by the Troops, the Enemy opened upon us a heavy fire of musketry from the Capitol and two other houses, these were therefore almost immediately Stormed by our People, taken possession of, and set on fire, after which the Town submitted without further resistance.

The Enemy himself on our entering the Town set Fire to the Navy Yard, (filled with Naval Stores) a Frigate of the largest class almost ready for Launching, and a Sloop of War laying off it, as he also did to the Fort which protected the Sea approach to Washington.

On taking Possession of the City we also set fire to the Presidents Palace, the Treasury, and the War Office, and in the morning Captain Wainwright went with a Party to see that the Destruction in the Navy Yard was Complete, when he destroyed whatever Stores and Buildings had

escaped the Flames of the preceding Night. A large quantity of Ammunition and ordnance Stores were likewise destroyed by us in the Arsenal, as were about Two hundred pieces of Artillery of different calibers, as well as a Vast quantity of small Arms. Two Rope Walks of a very extensive Nature, full of Tar, Rope &c. Situated at a considerable distance from the Yard were likewise set Fire to and consumed, in short Sir I do not believe a vestige of Public Property, or a Store of any kind which could be converted to the use of the Government, escaped Destruction; the Bridges across the Eastern Branch and the Potomac were likewise destroyed.

This general devastation being completed during the day of the 25th. we marched again at Nine that night on our Return by Bladensburg to upper Marlborough. We arrived yesterday Evening at the latter without molestation of any sort, indeed without a Single Musket having been fired, and this Morning we moved on to this place where I have found His Majesty's Sloop Manly, the Tenders, and the Boats, and I have hoisted my Flag pro tempore in the former. The Troops will probably march tomorrow or the next day at farthest to Benedict for re-embarkation, and this Flotilla will of course join you at the same time.

In closing Sir my Statement to you of the Arduous and highly important operations of this last week, I have a most pleasing duty to perform in assuring You of the good conduct of the Officers and Men who have been Serving under me. I have been particularly indebted whilst on this Service to Captain Wainwright of the Tonnant for the assistance he has invariably afforded me, and to Captains Palmer and Money for their Exertions during the March to and from Washington.

To Captain Nourse who has commanded the Flotilla during my absence, my acknowledgements are also most justly due, as well as to Captains Sullivan, Badcock, Somerville, Ramsay and Bruce who have acted in it under him.

Lieutenant James Scott now 1st. Lieutenant of the Albion has on this occasion Rendered me essential Services, and as I have had reason so often of late to mention to you the Gallant and Meritorious Conduct of this Officer, I trust you will permit me to seize this opportunity of recommending him particularly to your favorable Notice and Consideration.

Captain Robyns (the Senior Officer of Marines with the Fleet) who has had during these operations the Marines of the Ships united under his Orders, has executed ably and zealously the Several Services with which he has been entrusted, and is entitled to my best acknowledgements accordingly, *as is also Captain Harrison of the Marine Artillery who with the Officers and Men attached to him accompanied the Army to and from Washington.*

Mr. Dobie Surgeon of the Melpomene *volunteered his professional Services on this occasion and rendered much assistance to the wounded on the Field of Battle, as well as to many of the Men taken ill on the line of March.*

One Colonial Marine killed, One Master's Mate, Two Sergeants and Three Colonial Marines wounded, are the Casualties sustained by the Naval Department. A general List of the Killed and wounded of the whole Army will of course accompany the Reports of the Major General. I have the Honor to be Sir Your very faithful and Most Obedient and humble Servant

G. Cockburn Rear Admiral [33]

On August 28, the British captured Alexandria, Virginia, which surrendered without a fight. Over five days, the British raided warehouses and stores, but they agreed not to burn down the town. On the same day and with British naval guns trained on the town, Nantucket, Massachusetts, declared its neutrality and was spared from attack.

Last Months of 1814

On the evening of September 1, HMS *Avon*, an eighteen-gun brig sloop, was on patrol in the English Channel when she was spotted on the horizon by USS *Wasp*. The *Wasp* gave chase and after a lengthy interchange of broadsides, the badly damaged *Avon* was forced to surrender. Just as a prize crew was readying to go aboard, however, three more British warships were spotted, and the *Wasp* was forced to sail away. A short time later, the *Avon* sank.

Two days later, the USS *Tigress*, which was on station in Lake Huron to stop supplies from reaching Fort Michilimackinac, was boarded and quickly taken by a British force of sailors, soldiers, and warriors from the fort. On September 5, the USS *Scorpion*, which had been on patrol with the *Tigress*, returned and, unaware that the *Tigress* had been captured,

33. U.S. Naval History and Heritage Command, *The Defense and Burning of Washington in 1814*, "Battle of Bladensburg and the Attack on Washington, 24–25 August 1814," http://www.history.navy.mil/library/online/burning_washington.htm.

Thomas MacDonough
(print by
John Wesley Jarvis,
engraving by
Thomas Gimbrede)

came alongside. A British boarding party rushed on board and took the crew by surprise. The *Tigress* became HMS *Surprise*, and the *Scorpion* was renamed HMS *Confiance*.

General George Prevost led his army south toward Plattsburgh, leaving on September 1, while a British naval squadron under Captain George Downie sailed across Lake Champlain to take up position off Plattsburgh, arriving much later than expected. The American garrison was commanded by Brigadier General Alexander Macomb, while the American squadron was under the command of Master Commandant Thomas MacDonough.

Prevost, who was not a popular general, had more than eleven thousand men under his command, many of them experienced soldiers who had fought against Napoleon. Macomb had 1,500 regulars, mostly recruits or ill, and about two thousand largely untrained militia from New York and Vermont. Most of his able-bodied troops had been sent to defend Sackets Harbor. Almost all of the three thousand citizens of Plattsburgh had left the town fearing a British victory.

Macomb put his troops to work strengthening his defenses, while MacDonough prepared his squadron. In the previous months, the American shipyard at Otter Creek, Vermont, had launched the twenty-six-gun corvette USS *Saratoga*, the fourteen-gun schooner USS *Ticonderoga*, and the twenty-gun brig USS *Eagle*. Together with the seven-gun sloop USS *Preble*, the Americans had naval superiority. The British had built the thirty-six-gun frigate HMS *Confiance* (not the same as the renamed *Scorpion* mentioned above), but when it went into action, it was still unfinished and its crew untrained.

Captain Thomas
MacDonough
(oil by unknown artist)

As the British advanced, Macomb sent a column of 450 men to harass them. They would attack, fall back, block roads, burn bridges, and even change place and street names to delay the enemy.

Prevost reached Plattsburgh on September 6, but the Americans had destroyed the bridge across the Saranac River, which lay between the advancing British and the American defensive lines. Several attempts to cross the river on September 7 failed, so Prevost called up his artillery. The Americans replied by firing red-hot cannonballs at buildings in Plattsburgh where the British were positioned. The buildings caught fire and the British had to fall back even further. Prevost's scouts found a ford across the river, but he refused to attack until Downie's ships arrived. He argued that the Americans would have little fight left in them once their ships had been sunk.

While waiting for Downie and his ships, MacDonough drilled his crews in close-range combat. Knowing that he was outgunned by the British long guns, he anchored in Plattsburgh Bay so that the British would have to come in after him and the battle would be fought at

MacDonough's Farmhouse on Cumberland Bay, Lake Champlain
(print by unknown artist)

close quarters. Before dawn on September 11, the British fleet attacked. A broadside from *Confiance* killed or wounded a fifth of the *Saratoga*'s crew, but the return broadside killed Downie. The battle raged for about an hour until the *Confiance* surrendered. HMS *Chubb* and *Linnet* had already surrendered, and many of the British gunboats stayed out of the action.

Prevost ordered the land attack when he heard the naval guns firing, but when he was informed of the outcome, he ordered a full retreat, realizing he could not hold Plattsburgh without naval support. As night fell, Prevost started the march back to Canada—and many of his men deserted along the way.

It was a stunning victory for MacDonough, the "Hero of Lake Champlain," and the Americans. It gave them control of Lake Champlain and the leverage they needed to make demands at the peace talks in Ghent. Prevost was relieved of his command. He demanded a court-martial in order to clear his name, but died in 1816 before it could be held.

On September 4, Major Zachary Taylor and a force of 350 men were on their way by boat to evacuate the garrison at Prairie du Chien when they were attacked by pro-British Sauk warriors at Rock Island Rapids. Two sentries were killed overnight, and on September 5 three British

Naval War Heroes of the Battle of Lake Champlain
(lithograph by Nathaniel Currier)

MacDonough's Victory on Lake Champlain
(print by Henry Reinagle, engraving by Benjamin Tanner)

MacDonough's Victory on Lake Champlain
(watercolor by Edward Tufnell)

Battle of Plattsburgh (engraving by Read)

gunboats opened fire on them off Credit Island, injuring eleven sailors. Taylor was forced to withdraw downstream.

On September 8, Taylor started work on Fort Johnson, overlooking the Mississippi and Des Moines rivers in Illinois. The fort was built in record time and housed a company of men, but had to be abandoned in late October because no supplies arrived.

There were numerous skirmishes between American troops and militiamen as the British retreated following the Battle of Plattsburgh. On September 6, there was a skirmish at Beekmantown, New York, when British troops ran into a group of militia.

On September 9, the British captured and destroyed Fort O'Brien, in Machiasport, Maine.

The Battle of North Point, Maryland, on September 12 was technically a British victory, but it did help slow their advance on the strategically important port of Baltimore, giving the city more time to defend itself. The Maryland militia, commanded by General John Stricker, faced General Ross, who commanded 4,700 men—a brigade from the Duke of Wellington's Peninsular War army as well as a battalion of Royal Marines. The Americans posted riflemen well ahead of their main defensive lines, and one of Stricker's snipers killed Ross before the battle began. Colonel Arthur Brooke then took command.

The initial British attack was cut down by the accuracy of the riflemen and the cannons, which were firing rocks, nails, and horseshoes to inflict heavy casualties. The British then sent a second column to outflank the

Americans, and this broke through their lines. Stricker retreated back to Baltimore, but Brooke did not give chase. It was getting dark, and his men had suffered many more casualties than the Americans.

The Battle of Baltimore began on September 13 when the British started a naval bombardment of Fort McHenry and 4,300 British troops attacked the heavily fortified Hampstead Hill, where the Americans had more than ten cannons and over ten thousand troops. The British had planned to knock out Fort McHenry and then use its naval guns to attack Hampstead Hill. However, the Americans had deliberately sunk a number of merchant ships near the entrance to Baltimore Harbor to block any British passage, and the fort's gunners kept the Royal Navy warships at bay so they were unable to support Brooke's troops. The British fired more than 1,500 cannonballs at the fort, but caused little damage.

On the morning of September 14, a huge, new American flag—thirty feet by forty-two feet—was flying over the fort replacing the one that had been shot to pieces during the battle. The defense of Fort McHenry was the inspiration for Francis Scott Key's poem. Originally called "The Defense of Fort McHenry," it was set to music and renamed as "The Star-Spangled Banner," which became the national anthem in 1931.

Brooke, heavily outnumbered and without naval support, called off the attack and ordered his men back to the ships, which then set sail for New Orleans.

At the same time, the British were also attacking Fort Bowyer near Mobile, Alabama. The fort had been built by the Americans after Spanish troops left Mobile in April 1813. Captain William Percy of the Royal Navy wanted to capture the fort before advancing on Mobile in order to blockade Louisiana's trading routes. On the morning of September 12, Percy had landed a unit of Royal Marines plus about seven hundred Spanish mercenaries and warriors about nine miles east of the fort. The land attack on September 14 was repulsed, and on September 15, Percy started a naval bombardment. HMS *Hermes* ran aground and the crew scuttled her. The remaining three ships moved away to anchor overnight, and the next morning they left. The battle was not a major one, but it persuaded the British to focus elsewhere—and they set their sights on New Orleans.

On September 17, American troops who had been under siege in

Attack on the *General Armstrong* in Fayal Harbor, Azores
(print by Carlton T. Chapman)

Fort Erie since August 1 launched two raiding parties to capture British gun batteries. They managed to capture two batteries and destroy some of the siege guns before being forced back to the fort. Many of the Americans who took part in the raids were killed, injured, or captured. Ironically, the British commander had given the order to lift the siege the day before, and they were merely waiting for draft animals to arrive or else they would already have started to leave. The British finally left on September 21.

On September 26, the American privateer *General Armstrong* was taking on supplies in the neutral port of Faial in the Azores when three British warships—the *Plantagenet*, *Rota*, and *Carnation*—sailed into the harbor and tried to board the American ship. In the ensuing battles, two hundred British sailors were killed and just two Americans. The British commander Robert Lloyd was under orders to make all haste to join the flotilla in the Caribbean being assembled to attack New Orleans and should not in any case have attacked the American ship in a neutral

Privateer *General Armstrong*
(lithograph by Nathaniel Currier)

harbor. However, he claimed that two of the *General Armstrong*'s crew were deserters from his ship.

On October 19, the Battle of Cook's Mills took place near present-day Welland, Ontario. It was the last battle between the British and Americans along the Niagara River. After lifting the siege of Fort Erie, General Drummond withdrew to Fort Chippawa. American troops under Major General George Izard, who had been sent from Plattsburgh to reinforce Fort Erie, marched north to Chippawa Creek. The Americans captured a British supply depot at Cook's Mills and took up defensive positions in the woods. The British attacked, but could not draw the Americans out and eventually withdrew.

On October 21, news of the Battle of Plattsburgh and other setbacks having reached London, the British government offered peace on the basis of *uti possidetis*, which literally means that both sides get to keep what they possess at that moment in time. The Americans rejected this, and the British later withdrew their insistence for it on November 27, opening the way for a peace deal to be hammered out.

During October, a force of about seven hundred American troops, led by Brigadier General Duncan McArthur, had left Detroit to carry out raids on settlements in the Thames Valley that supplied British troops in Upper Canada. On November 5, McArthur arrived at Brant's Ford on

Admiral Cochrane
(print by
unknown artist)

the Grand River and was met by Canadian militia and warriors. Shots were fired and, hearing that reinforcements were coming from Burlington Heights, McArthur rode south to raid settlements along the north shore of Lake Erie as he headed back to Detroit.

Although the siege had been lifted, the American garrison abandoned Fort Erie on November 5 and withdrew to Buffalo. The fort was running short of supplies and winter was coming, so Izard blew the fort up. It was never rebuilt.

On November 25, a British invasion fleet carrying more than ten thousand soldiers, under the command of Admiral Sir Alexander Cochrane, sailed from Jamaica for New Orleans.

Knowing that the British fleet was nearing New Orleans, the Americans started to gather as many vessels as they could to block the advance. A small flotilla of eight American gunboats was sent to patrol Lake Borgne in the approaches to New Orleans.

Admiral Cochrane sent forty-two armed longboats, launches, and barges, three gigs, and 1,200 men to find and destroy the defenders. On the morning of December 14, after finishing their breakfast, the British closed in and started to board the American vessels. The entire American flotilla was captured or scuttled. However, although the British won the battle, it delayed them, giving General Jackson much-needed time to prepare his defenses.

On December 23, the first wave of British troops landed and reached

Signing of the Treaty of Ghent
(Sir Amedee Forestier)

the east bank of the Mississippi River about nine miles south of New Orleans. Rather than press on, they made camp for the night at Lacoste's Plantation. Under the cover of darkness, Jackson led about 2,100 men and attacked the camp, inflicting heavy losses. Although the British did not fall back, they were not inclined to advance either, and Jackson gained two extra days to further fortify his defenses.

On December 25, General Edward Pakenham held a council of war with General John Keane and Admiral Cochrane. Three days later, he sent a strong force to probe the Americans' defensive lines. They reported back that the Americans' earthworks were not protected by significant artillery. However, as soon as the British withdrew, Jackson started work on a series of gun batteries along his defensive line. The battle for New Orleans would begin in earnest with the new year.

Meanwhile, on December 24, unknown to the combatants in North America, the Treaty of Ghent was signed, officially ending the war between Britain and the United States, although it still had to be ratified by both governments—a process that was to take weeks.

Another peace effort was ongoing in Hartford, Connecticut, as well.

The Treaty of Ghent

EFFORTS TO END THE WAR began in 1812 when the chief U.S. diplomat in London proposed an armistice in return for ending impressments; the British refused. Later in 1812, when the British captured Detroit and news of the repeal of the Orders in Council reached Washington, Sir George Prevost arranged an armistice with his counterpart Henry Dearborn. However, President James Madison decided to continue the war.

In 1813, Russia offered to mediate a peace, but London rejected the offer because it might compromise British interests in Europe. Great Britain and the United States agreed to commence peace negotiations in January 1814, but the talks were delayed.

Finally, in August 1814, peace discussions began in Ghent, a city in neutral Belgium. Both sides started out with impossible demands, but as the talks dragged on, it became clear that neither side wanted to prolong the war and their best interests were served by making peace and becoming trading partners again. Great Britain and the United States agreed to return to the status quo as it was before the war, and the Treaty of Ghent was signed on December 24, 1814. It was formally ratified by both sides in February 1815.

The five New England states had opposed the war from the start, and by the end of 1814 it was so unpopular that a convention was called. The Hartford Convention convened on December 15 and sat until January 4. At secret meetings, delegates called for secession from the United States, although this was never publicly stated. The Battle of New Orleans and the signing of the Treaty of Ghent negated anything the convention had called for, however, and sounded the death knell for the Federalist Party.

SIX

1815

ON JANUARY 1, 1815, the British attacked the American lines in New Orleans with artillery, and fire was returned. After three hours, the British ran out of ammunition, and General Pakenham decided to wait for the rest of his force—eight thousand men—to arrive before attacking. What he didn't know was that the artillery barrage had forced Jackson's troops on the left of the line to retreat from their positions. Had Pakenham sent his army through this hole in the defensive lines right away, they probably would have won the day.

Pakenham finally ordered his army to attack in a pincer movement on January 8. A fast-moving column was to wipe out the American batteries, while the main force was to make a frontal attack against General Jackson's defensive line. The column got bogged down in thick mud, however, and finally set off more than twelve hours late. The main force attacked before dawn under the cover of fog, but as they neared the American positions, the fog lifted and the British were cut down by the American batteries, which the British had not been able to silence. Many of their senior officers were killed, which led to more confusion on the battlefield. The American defensive earthworks were so well fortified that few British troops were able to breach them, and when they did, they were either shot or captured.

General Pakenham and his second in command General Samuel Gibbs were both killed by grapeshot. The British troops, not knowing whether to advance or retreat, waited in the open while they were blasted by American artillery. Eventually General John Lambert assumed command

The Battle of New Orleans
(print of an engraving by unknown artist)

The Battle of New Orleans
(lithograph by Hyacinthe Laclotte)

Battle between USS *President*, HMS *Endymion* and *Pomone*
(hand-colored engraving by unknown artist)

and ordered an immediate retreat. The Battle of New Orleans was the most decisive battle of the war and America's greatest land victory.

On January 9, British warships attacked Fort St. Philip, which had been built on the Mississippi River to protect New Orleans from a naval attack from the Gulf of Mexico. The fort was besieged for ten days, during which it was under a steady naval bombardment. On January 18, the British ships ceased firing, and the following day called off the siege and sailed away.

On January 16, the USS *President*, which had been blockaded in New York harbor, tried to break out during a gale but ran into a squadron of four British warships—HMS *Majestic*, *Endymion*, *Pomone*, and *Tenedos*. The *President* had been badly damaged during the breakout when she got stuck on a sandbar at the mouth of the harbor for two hours and was unable to sail at top speed. She was overtaken by the *Endymion*, and the two ships traded broadsides. As the two ships battled it out, *Pomone*

The Chase of the USS *President*
(print by Carlton T. Chapman)

The USS *President*
(print by Jean Jerome Baugean)

USS *President* in Action against HMS *Endymion*
(print of an engraving by Thomas Buttersworth)

and *Tenedos* appeared and Commodore Stephen Decatur, the *President's* captain, was forced to surrender. The damaged *Endymion* limped to Bermuda with her prize.

On February 1, the British started construction of the Pentanguishene Naval Yard in Ontario to build gunboats and brigs to replenish the British Great Lakes fleet. News of the Treaty of Ghent had still not reached the Americas.

Having failed to take New Orleans, the British turned their attention on Mobile and, on February 12, attacked Fort Bowyer. After the first attack in September 1814, Jackson had strengthened its fortifications and increased the garrison. But a British force with heavy artillery attacked the fort from the land, its weakest side. After a punishing barrage, the Americans surrendered. It was at this point that the HMS *Brazen* arrived with news of the Treaty of Ghent. The British troops who had been readying to attack Mobile promptly boarded their ships and sailed home.

The Treaty of Ghent was unanimously approved by the U.S. Senate on February 16 and signed by President James Madison on February 17, bringing the war to an official close.

However, the word still had not reached all the ships at sea. On February 20, HMS *Cyane* and *Levant* were captured by the USS *Constitution*, under the command of Captain Charles Stewart, after a battle off the Atlantic coast of Africa. While the two British warships tried to attack Old Ironsides together, the *Constitution* took on the *Cyane* first and its well-trained gunners caused major damage. The *Constitution* then turned her broadsides on the *Levant*, and both British warships surrendered. The three ships were sailing back to the United States when they were chased by a British squadron. The *Constitution* and her prize HMS *Cyane* escaped, while the *Levant* was retaken by the British.

The battle between these three vessels is described here in Captain Stewart's official log.

Minutes of Action between the U.S. Frigate Constitution *and*
H.M. Ships Cyane *and* Levant,
20 February 1815

Commences with light breezes from the E and cloudy weather. At 1
discovered a sail two points on the larboard bow. Hauled up and made

Captain Charles Stewart
(print by
Joseph Wood)

*sail in chase. At 1/2 past 1 made the Sail to be a Ship's at 3/4 past 1
discovered another Sail ahead. Made them out at 2 p.m. to be both Ships,
standing close hauled, with their Starboard tacks on board. At 4 p.m. the
weathermost ship made signals and bore up for her consort, then about
ten miles to the leeward. We bore up after her, and set lower topmast, top
gallant, and royal studding sails in chase. At 1/2 past 4 carried away our
main royal mast. Took in the Sails and got another prepared. At 5 p.m.
commenced firing on the chase from our larboard bow guns. Our shot falling
short, ceased firing. At 1/2 past 5, finding it impossible to prevent their
junction, cleared ship for action, then about 4 miles from the two ships.
At 40 minutes after 5, they passed within hail of each other, and hauled
by the wind on the starboard tack, hauled up their courses and prepared
to receive us. At 45 minutes past 5, they made all sail close hauled by the
wind, in hopes of getting to windward of us. At 55 minutes past 5, finding
themselves disappointed in their object, and we were closing with them
fast, they shortened sail and formed on a line of wind, about half a cables
length from each other. At 6 p.m. having them under the command of our
battery, hoisted our colours, which was answered by both ships hoisting
English Ensigns. At 5 minutes past 6, ranged up on the Starboard side
of the Sternmost Ship, about 200 yards distant, and commenced action by
broadsides, both ships returning fire with great spirit for about 12 minutes,*

Action between USS *Constitution* and HMS *Cyane* and *Levant*
(print by Carlton T. Chapman)

*then the fire of the enemy beginning to slacken, and the great column of
smoke collected under our lee, induced us to cease our fire to ascertain their
positions and conditions. In about 3 minutes, the smoke clearing away, we
found ourselves abreast of their headmost ship, the sternmost ship luffing up
for our larboard quarter. We poured a broadside into the headmost ship, and
then braced aback our Main and Mizzen Topsails, and backed astern under
the cover of smoke, abreast the stern most ship, when action was continued
with spirit and considerable effect until 35 minutes past 6, when the enemy's
fire again slackened, and we discovered the headmost bearing up—filled
our topsails—shot ahead, and gave her two stern rakes. We then discovered
the sternmost ship nearing also. Wore ship immediately after her, and gave
her a stern rake, she luffing too on our Starboard bows, and giving us her
larboard broadside. We ranged up on the larboard quarter, within hail, and
was about to give her our starboard broadside when she struck her colours,
fired a lee gun, and yielded. At 20 minutes past 6, took possession of H.M.
Ship Cyane, Captain Gordon Falcon, mounting 34 guns At 8 p.m. filled
away after her consort, which was still in sight to leeward. At 1/2 past
8 found her standing towards us, with her Starboard tacks close hauled,
with top-gallant set, and colours flying. At 20 minutes past 8, ranged close
along to windward of her, on opposite tacks, and exchanged broadsides.*

Capture of HMS *Cyane* and *Levant* by USS *Constitution*

Wore immediately under her stern and raked her with a broadside, she then crowded all sail and endeavored to escape by running. Hauled on board our Tacks, Let Spanker and Flying jib in chase. At 1/2 past 9 commenced firing on her from our starboard bow chaser. Gave her several shot which cut her spars and rigging considerably. At 10 p.m. finding they could not escape, fired a gun, struck her colours and yielded. We immediately took possession of H.M. Ship Levant, Honorable Captain George Douglas, mounting 21 guns. At 1 a.m. the damages of our rigging was repaired, sails and the ship in fighting condition.[34]

On March 1, Napoleon escaped from exile on Elba and returned to France, giving the British even more incentive to get their warships and troops back to Europe as quickly as possible.

On March 23, HMS *Penguin* was captured by the USS *Hornet* off Tristan da Cunha in the South Atlantic. The engagement lasted twenty-two minutes, during which the *Penguin*'s captain, Commander James Dickinson, was killed. The *Penguin* was scuttled the next day, as she was too badly damaged to save. It was the last naval engagement of the war—more than a month after the war was officially over.

The Battle of the Sink Hole on May 24 was the last known land battle of the war, fought between Missouri Rangers and Sauk Indians led by Black Hawk near the mouth of the Cuivre River in Missouri. The Sauk ambushed the Rangers, but despite heavier casualties, the Americans won the day.

---

34. Enclosure in Captain Stephen Decatur's letter to Secretary of the Navy Benjamin Crowninshield, dated May 1814, National Archives, Record Group 45, Captain's Letters, 1815, Vol. 3, No. 93.

SEVEN

PEACE

ALTHOUGH THE WAR had almost bankrupted the nation, the peace did lead to a new era of prosperity and expansion for the United States. The British hope of establishing a Native American buffer zone west of the Mississippi vanished after their defeat at the Battle of New Orleans, when various treaties with Native American tribes secured vast tracts of land for the United States. American settlers headed further west, claiming new territory as they went. Had the British won the Battle of New Orleans and reneged on the Treaty of Ghent, this westward expansion would not have been possible, and the United States today might still exist mainly east of the Mississippi.

Opposition to the war led to the New England states' talk about secession, but news of the battles of New Orleans and Baltimore led to a new wave of national patriotism and helped unite the country. People who talked of secession were branded as traitors, and the Federalist Party, which had supported such a move, was destroyed politically because of it.

Two of the war's most successful generals—Andrew Jackson and William Henry Harrison—were later elected president of the United States because of their continued popularity.

The blockade during the war forced the Americans to manufacture many of the goods they traditionally imported and there was an industrial boom after the war.

The war also helped unite the nation's fighting forces. State and territorial militias overcame their differences to fight the common enemy together. After the war, the importance of a well-trained cadre of senior officers was recognized, and the U.S. Military Academy at West Point was reorganized to achieve this. Gradually, militias ceded their responsibility for defense to the U.S. Army. A nationwide program was started to construct new forts and strengthen those already built, especially along the Mississippi and in the new territories. One of the aims of the forts was to protect the growing numbers of settlers heading west, and this also meant removing the Native American tribes in their way. This became a top priority of the U.S. government.

The U.S. Navy came out of the war with perhaps the most kudos. It had taken on the most powerful navy in the world—the Royal Navy—and come out victorious on several occasions. Its officers developed new battle techniques, some of which were later adopted by the British. The war also convinced the U.S. Congress that a strong and well-trained navy was in the national interest—as, of course, it still is.

For the British, the war was an expensive diversion from the Napoleonic Wars then being fought in Europe, and for that reason it is seldom mentioned in history books published in the United Kingdom. The Royal Navy and Admiralty were acutely embarrassed at both their defeat by a fledgling American navy and their inability to protect British merchant ships, many of which were captured by American warships and privateers. The British navy did score some notable sea victories and was successful in blockading U.S. ports to prevent trade, but it had far more ships to start with and did not use this superiority to best advantage.

Likewise, the highly trained British army suffered several major defeats to an American army that was often ill trained and ill equipped. The difference was, of course, that the Americans were fighting for their freedom. Another reason for many of the British setbacks was the quality of their leadership. Many of the most experienced generals were fighting in Europe, and the caliber of senior officers sent to North America was not always of the highest. The British did not consider the Americans to be a serious problem at first and thought they would have a rapid and overwhelming victory in the war.

The Canadians welcomed the end of the war, but they were not yet ready to seek independence. The war had shown them how vulnerable they would be to American troops without a strong British presence to protect them. In fact, the support they received from the British, especially with the troop reinforcements in 1814, increased their loyalty to Britain. This in turn led to opposition to the continued immigration of American settlers into the Canadian colonies, because many of them argued for integration with the United States. If American settlers had continued to emigrate to the Canadian colonies in large numbers, they might have achieved this before the spirit of Canadian nationalism developed. The seeds of nationalism had been sown, however, and in 1867 Upper and Lower Canada merged to become the Canadian Confederation.

Another outcome of the war was that the British realized how dependent they were on the St. Lawrence River for supplies. Had the Americans blocked the river early on in the war, supplies would have not been able to reach Upper Canada, and Britain would likely have been forced to withdraw, effectively handing over the territory to the Americans. After the war, they started construction of the Rideau Canal linking Kingston on Lake Ontario to the Ottawa River, thus providing an alternate supply route—though it was never needed. The settlement that grow up where the canal joined the Ottawa River became Ottawa.

The biggest losers were the Native Americans. Before the war, they controlled almost all the land west of the Mississippi and, supported by the British, harassed any attempts by American settlers to move west. With Britain and America at peace, the Indians lost the protection of the British. The Creek in the south had already been decimated by General Jackson at the Battle of Horseshoe Bend, which opened up huge areas for settlement in Alabama and Georgia. In the north, the British agreed not to arm the Native Americans, and American settlers moved in ever larger numbers westward.

REFERENCES

Allen, Joseph. *Battles of the British Navy*, Vol. 2. London: Henry G. Bohn, 1852.

Beirne, Francis F. *The War of 1812*. New York: Dutton, 1949. Reprint, Hamden, CT: Archon Books, 1965.

Berube, Claude G., and John Rodgaard. *A Call to the Sea: Captain Charles Stewart of the USS* Constitution. Dulles, VA: Potomac Books, 2005.

Bird, Harrison. *Navies in the Mountains: The Battles on the Waters of Lake Champlain and Lake George, 1609–1814*. New York: Oxford University Press, 1962.

Brown, Wilburt S. *The Amphibious Campaign for West Florida and Louisiana, 1814–1815: A Critical Review of Strategy and Tactics at New Orleans*. University: University of Alabama Press, 1969.

Byron, Gilbert. *The War of 1812 on the Chesapeake Bay*. Baltimore: Maryland Historical Society, 1964.

Cooper, James Fenimore. *Ned Myers; or, A Life before the Mast*. With annotations by W. S. Dudley. Annapolis, MD: Naval Institute Press, 1989.

Cranwell, John P., and William B. Crane. *Men of Marque: A History of Private Armed Vessels Out of Baltimore during the War of 1812*. New York: Norton, 1940.

Crawford, Michael J., and Christine E. Hughes. *The Reestablishment of the Navy, 1787–1801: Historical Overview and Select Bibliography*. Naval History Biographies, No. 4. Washington, DC: Naval Historical Center, Department of the Navy, 1995.

Dillon, Richard. *We Have Met the Enemy: Oliver Hazard Perry, Wilderness Commodore*. New York: McGraw-Hill, 1978.

Drake, Frederick C. "Commodore Sir James Yeo and Governor General George Prevost: A Study in Command Relations, 1813–14." In *New Interpretations in Naval History: Selected Papers from the Eighth Naval History Symposium*, edited by William B. Cogar, 156–71. Annapolis, MD: Naval Institute Press, 1989.

Dudley, William S. "Commodore Isaac Chauncey and U.S. Joint Operations on Lake Ontario, 1813–14." In *New Interpretations in Naval History: Selected*

Papers from the Eighth Naval History Symposium, edited by William B. Cogar, 139–55. Annapolis, MD: Naval Institute Press, 1989.

Dudley, William S., and Michael J. Crawford, eds. *The Naval War of 1812: A Documentary History*. 3 vols. Washington, DC: Naval Historical Center, 1985–2002.

Durand, James R. *James Durand, an Able Seaman of 1812: His Adventures on "Old Ironsides," and as an Impressed Sailor in the British Navy*. Edited by George S. Brooks. New Haven, CT: Yale University Press, 1926.

Dutton, Charles J. *Oliver Hazard Perry*. New York: Longmans, Green, 1935.

Eckert, Edward K. *The Navy Department in the War of 1812*. University of Florida Social Sciences Monograph, No. 48. Gainesville: University of Florida Press, 1973.

Eller, Ernest M., William J. Morgan, and Richard M. Basoco. *Sea Power and the Battle of New Orleans*. New Orleans: Landmark Society, 1965.

Everest, Allan S. *The War of 1812 in the Champlain Valley*. Syracuse, NY: Syracuse University Press, 1981.

Forester, Cecil S. *The Age of Fighting Sail: The Story of the Naval War of 1812*. Garden City, NY: Doubleday, 1956.

Garitee, Jerome R. *The Republic's Private Navy: The American Privateering Business as Practiced by Baltimore during the War of 1812*. American Maritime Library, Vol. 8. Middletown, CT: Published for Mystic Seaport by Wesleyan University Press, 1977.

Gleaves, Albert. *James Lawrence, Captain, United States Navy, Commander of the Chesapeake*. New York: Putnam, 1904.

Grant, Bruce. *Isaac Hull, Captain of Old Ironsides*. Chicago: Pellegrini & Cudahy, 1947.

Hickey, Donald R. *The War of 1812: A Forgotten Conflict*. Urbana: University of Illinois Press, 1989.

Hitsman, J. Mackay. *The Incredible War of 1812: A Military History*. Toronto: University of Toronto Press, 1965.

Horsman, Reginald. *The Causes of the War of 1812*. Philadelphia: University of Pennsylvania Press, 1962.

Howe, Daniel Walker. *What Hath God Wrought: The Transformation of America*. New York: Oxford University Press, 2007.

Hull, Isaac. *Commodore Hull: Papers of Isaac Hull, Commodore, United States Navy*. Edited by Gardner W. Allen. Boston: Boston Athenaeum, 1929.

Jones, Noah. *Journals of Two Cruises aboard the American Privateer* Yankee, *by a Wanderer*. New York: Macmillan, 1967.

Long, David F. *Nothing Too Daring: A Biography of Commodore David Porter, 1780–1843*. Annapolis, MD: U.S. Naval Institute, 1970.

Lossing, Benson J. *Pictorial Field-Book of the War of 1812*. New York: Harper, 1868.

Mackenzie, Alexander S. *Life of Stephen Decatur, a Commodore in the Navy of the United States*. Boston: Little, Brown, 1846.

Mahan, Alfred T. *Sea Power in Its Relations to the War of 1812.* 2 vols. Boston: Little, Brown, 1905. Reprint, New York: Greenwood Press, 1968; New York: Haskell House, 1969.

Mahon, John K. *The War of 1812.* Gainesville: University of Florida Press, 1972.

Maloney, Linda M. *The Captain from Connecticut: The Life and Naval Times of Isaac Hull.* Boston: Northeastern University Press, 1986.

———. "The War of 1812: What Role for Sea Power?" In *In Peace and War: Interpretations of American Naval History, 1775–1984,* 2nd ed., edited by Kenneth J. Hagan, 46–62. Westport, CT: Greenwood Press, 1984.

McClellan, Edwin N. "The Navy at the Battle of New Orleans." [U.S. Naval Institute] *Proceedings* 50 (December 1924): 2041–60.

Miller, Nathan. *The U.S. Navy: A History.* Annapolis, MD: Naval Institute Press, 1997.

Mills, James C. *Oliver Hazard Perry and the Battle of Lake Erie.* Detroit: J. Phelps, 1913.

Muller, Charles G. *The Darkest Day: 1814; The Washington-Baltimore Campaign.* Philadelphia: Lippincott, 1963.

Pack, James. *The Man Who Burned the White House: Admiral Sir George Cockburn, 1772–1853.* Annapolis, MD: Naval Institute Press, 1987.

Poolman, Kenneth. *Guns off Cape Ann: The Story of the* Shannon *and the* Chesapeake. Chicago: Rand McNally, 1962.

Porter, David. *Journal of a Cruise Made to the Pacific Ocean, by Captain David Porter, in the United States Frigate* Essex, *in the Years 1812, 1813, and 1814.* New York: Wiley & Halstead, 1815. 2 vols. Reprint, Annapolis, MD: Naval Institute Press, 1987; Cranbury, NJ: Scholars Bookshelf, 2006.

Pullen, Hugh F. *The* Shannon *and the* Chesapeake. Toronto: McClelland & Stewart, 1970.

Roosevelt, Theodore. *The Naval War of 1812; or, The History of the United States Navy during the Last War with Great Britain: To Which Is Appended an Account of the Battle of New Orleans,* 6th ed. New York: Putnam, 1897. Reprint (1883 ed.), New York: Haskell House, 1969.

Shomette, Donald G. *Flotilla: Battle for the Patuxent.* Solomons, MD: Calvert Marine Museum Press, 1981.

Skaggs, David Curtis. "Joint Operations during the Detroit–Lake Erie Campaign, 1813." In *New Interpretations in Naval History: Selected Papers from the Eighth Naval History Symposium,* edited by William B. Cogar, 121–38. Annapolis. MD: Naval Institute Press, 1989.

Stewart, Richard W., ed. *American Military History,* Vol. 1: *The United States Army and the Forging of a Nation, 1775–1917.* Army Historical Series, CMH Pub. 30-21. Washington, DC: Center of Military History, U.S. Army.

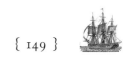

INDEX